B A T T L E F I E L D   B R I T A I N

# BATTLES OF THE
# SCOTTISH
# LOWLANDS

MAC MILLAN

BATTLEFIELD BRITAIN

# BATTLES OF THE SCOTTISH LOWLANDS

## STUART REID

Pen & Sword
**MILITARY**

First published in Great Britain in 2004 by
PEN & SWORD MILITARY
an imprint of
Pen & Sword Books Limited
47 Church Street
Barnsley
South Yorkshire
S70 2AS

ISBN: 1 84415 078 X

Typeset in 9pt Palatino by Pen & Sword Books Limited

Printed and bound in England by
CPI UK

*Pen & Sword Books incorporates the imprints of*
Pen & Sword Aviation, Pen & Sword Maritime,, Pen & Sword Military,
Wharncliffe Local History, Pen & Sword Select,
Pen & Sword Military Classics and Leo Cooper

*For a complete list of Pen & Sword titles please contact:*
PEN & SWORD BOOKS LIMITED
47 Church Street, Barnsley, South Yorkshire, S70 2AS, England
email: enquiries@pen-and-sword.co.uk • website: www.pen-and-sword.co.uk

# Contents

# Maps

Map key

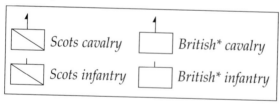

*Scots cavalry*    *British\* cavalry*

*Scots infantry*    *British\* infantry*

*\* English*

All unit frontages in the maps are to scale although depths of formations are exaggerated for the sake of clarity.

# Introduction

This is a book about Scotland's military history, told through a triptych of nine battles: three from the medieval period, three from the Civil Wars of the seventeenth century and three from the Jacobite risings of the eighteenth. Each part is preceded by a comprehensive essay describing the weapons, organisation and tactics of the day, which will help in understanding how the battles were actually fought.

Inevitably the decision to concentrate on just nine battles means that a great many others, including some well-known ones, have been left out. On the other hand, by deliberately avoiding the all-inclusive gazetteer approach, it has been possible to deal with each of the chosen battles properly and to provide completely new and fresh treatments of them, sometimes in far greater detail than has been possible before.

This particular volume covers Lowland Scotland, and the battles are no random selection, for while one battle from each part of the triptych – Pinkie 1547, Dunbar 1650 and Prestonpans 1745 – were fought in the eastern approaches to Edinburgh, the majority of those discussed in these pages were fought within a very short radius of Stirling Castle and Stirling Bridge. There was reason enough for this concentration of military activity and if this book has a central historical theme running through it, then it is the struggle to control this geographical choke-point and, by extension, Scotland itself.

In broad geographical terms Scotland is effectively split in two by the Firth of Forth, often referred to in medieval times as the Scottish Sea. Historically, Stirling Bridge was the lowest point at which the Forth could be crossed by an army and while there were a series of fords a short distance upstream, beyond its confluence with the River Teith, the routes to and from them were uncertain and in any case still dominated by the castle. The land further to the west, beyond the celebrated Fords of Frew, was a trackless wilderness.

Yet the choke-point worked both ways. At Stirling Bridge in 1297 an English army trying to come northwards was lured to its destruction, while, at Bannockburn in 1314, Stirling Castle itself was merely the bait in a trap set for an English army come to save it. Montrose's victory at Kilsyth in 1645 is something of an oddity for it was fought after he and his men had successfully evaded the troops guarding the main crossing point. Inverkeithing in 1651, on the other hand, represented a much bolder and even more successful attempt by an English army to outflank the Stirling defences by sailing across the Firth of Forth and landing on the Fife shore. Conversely when the Jacobite army tried the same trick in reverse in 1715, the initial success was not followed up and they were forced instead to mount a full blown frontal offensive towards Stirling which came to grief on Sheriffmuir. The last of the battles discussed here, Falkirk in 1746, was, like Bannockburn, fought against an army coming north to save Stirling Castle. But whilst Bruce won a crushing victory, Prince Charles Edward's army engaged in a remarkably faithful replay of the debacle at Sheriffmuir 30 years before, where it was famously remarked that everyone on both sides ran away.

Naturally enough this heavy concentration of battlefields in and around the immediate area of Stirling makes visiting them all the easier, although in the nature of things the area's strategic importance in commercial as well as military terms has also contributed to their partial loss to modern development. Nevertheless all of them are still worth visiting and if at first it seems that all has been buried under brick and concrete, lift up your eyes to the hills, for the setting and the broader landscape remains.

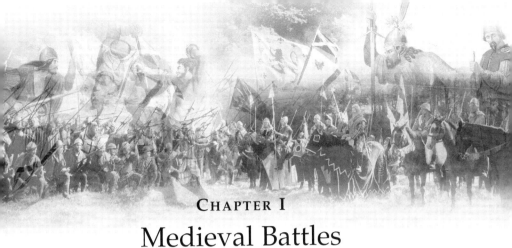

## Chapter I

# Medieval Battles

## Warriors: Schiltrons

From the very beginning the Scots were spearmen. The nobles, knights, bonnet lairds and burgesses who led them might have had more and better armour, and swords as well, but that merely fitted them to stand in the front ranks of the schiltrons; this evocative term which has been variously interpreted but which best translates as moving thickets – a veritable forests of pikes.

Scots law required every man between the traditional ages of sixteen and sixty to turn out in time of war, but most of them probably got no further than the local wapinschaw – weapon showing – where only those adjudged fit to bear 'arms defencible' were entered on the rolls – hence the term fencibles. Then, depending on the scale of the levy, one man in four or even one man in eight would actually be picked, thereby ensuring minimal disruption to the local economy and leaving a substantial reserve which could still be called upon in an emergency. In theory those men who were actually levied out were only bound to forty days' service. There was no question of course of their simply turning around again and heading for home at the expiry of those forty days. But if the campaign continued beyond that time the responsibility for feeding and maintaining them passed from the sherriffdom or royal burgh which had levied them out, to the Crown.

It is important to draw a distinction between what might be termed local and Royal levies, for only the latter were maintained in service long enough to receive proper training at unit level. The normal size for a body of infantry throughout military history has always been about 5-600 men whether it be called a schiltron, a regiment or a battalion, and, until the advent of the musket, they were normally formed up in six ranks, which was the optimum depth for both stability and manoeuvrability. Three or four of these self-contained units could be brigaded together under a single commander, but if they were then to move, let alone manoeuvre effectively without dissolving into a rabble, it was necessary to drill them – intensively.

Scots infantrymen were primarily armed with 3.6 metre (12 foot) spears which eventually evolved into long pikes. Their English counterparts on the other hand were generally armed with bills. These were relatively short weapons with large blades, whose resemblance to tin-openers was far from co-incidental, and which were extremely effective in hand-to-hand fighting. The Scots also used to them to a degree, but the evidence suggests that for so long as the momentum of the attack could be maintained the ordinary Scottish spear was more than effective enough to quite literally push back the opposing formation.

It is worth emphasising this pushing business, for while it might be expected that the pikes or spears might transfix those getting in their way it seems to have been a rare occurrence. Indeed if it were otherwise it would have been very hard to find anyone willing to stand in the forefront. Instead, a contemporary account of the Battle of Langside in 1568 provides an interesting description of what really happened when two bodies of pikemen met head on:

'...He and Grange, at the joining, cried to let their adversaries foot lay down their spears, to bear up theirs, which spears were so thick fixed in the others jacks, that some of the pistols and great staves, that were thrown by them which were behind, might be seen lying upon the spears... Grange reinforced that wing which was beginning to fly; which fresh men with their loose weapons struck the enemy in their flanks and faces, which forced them incontinent to give place and turn back and long fighting and pushing others to and fro with their spears... the only slaughter was at the first rencounter, by the shot of the soldiers which Grange had planted at the lane-head behind some dykes...'

It is also worth noting the emphasis placed on the fact that there were few casualties in the encounter, first because instead of transfixing the opposing soldiers, the pikes were lodged in their jacks – padded coats or jerkins – and secondly because Grange allowed the defeated side to get away. Ordinarily, if the scrum collapsed the victorious side would mercilessly set about the losers as they struggled to rise and flee. The fact of the matter was that despite its dramatic potential relatively few

## SCHILTRONS

The origin of the term Schiltron, also variously spelled schiltrum or schiltrone, is obscure. A strong body of opinion holds that it translates as a shield-round or shield-ring, but whilst at first sight attractive this interpretation is not supported by the evidence.

Shield-rings as used by Saxon and Norse warriors were a defensive formation protected by an interlocking 'wall' of large round shields. Scots pikemen on the other hand sometimes carried a small round shield or target, but this was very much a secondary weapon to be used with a sword when pikes were broken or discarded. Moreover with the notable exception of Wallace's debacle at Falkirk, the schiltron was not a 'round' defensive formation at all, but rather a dense line or column. Contemporary writers in fact use the term indiscriminately to describe any formation of infantry drawn up in close order.

A far likelier interpretation of the term therefore is that it is a composite of the old Scots word schilt or sclut which means to tread slowly and deliberately as men in formation must, and rone, which is an old term for a thicket. The moving forest or thicket of pikes is a frequently encountered similie, used to describe such formations in English sources, and may indeed also echo the famous advance of Birnam Wood on Dunsinane.

*A modern re-enactment of Scots pikemen drawn up in a schiltron below the Abbey Craig at Causewayhead.*

men were ever slain in hand-to-hand combat, but a great many were killed running away from it.

Should the momentum of the attack be lost however, as described at Langside, the handier bill then came into its own and from the English point of view therefore it was vital to bring the schiltrons to a halt as quickly as possible. At first it appeared that the natural solution was to ride them down with cavalry, of which English armies were always well provided, but it soon proved to be a chasteningly one-sided encounter and unless the schiltron was already in disorder the English cavalry invariably came off worse.

Indeed in looking at the relative effectiveness of pikemen and cavalrymen, the conclusion has to be that it was no contest. In theory a heavily armed knight should have no trouble whatever in riding down any number of infantrymen, but a formation of pikemen six ranks deep will quite literally present a veritable hedge of about a dozen spear-points, which a horse will invariably 'refuse'. A good rider might be still able to force a well schooled mount forward, but not with sufficient momentum to seriously disrupt the formation – as a surprising number of English knights time and again discovered the hard way.

A far more effective way of stopping the schiltrons soon proved to be the English longbow. Although the Scots also employed longbowmen they were never as effective as their southern counterparts, but it is important to note the near

## SITE OF THE
# BATTLE OF STIRLING BRIDGE

In early September 1297 a mighty army arrived in Stirling to put down Scots resistance to English rule. The Scots allowed around half the invaders to advance across the narrow bridge over the Forth. Then William Wallace and the Scots swept forward to achieve a brilliant victory over a far-superior force.

*The original wooden-piered Stirling Bridge as depicted on an old burgh seal.*

uniqueness of the English article. It is all too easy to see him as a humble peasant bringing down the mighty chivalry of France at Crécy, Poitiers and Agincourt, but in reality he was a well trained and equipped professional soldier. He had to be, for archery was certainly not a part-time occupation. Mastering a yew bow with a draw-weight of some 100lb required long training from boyhood and constant practice thereafter. He had to be in superb physical condition, well fed and possessed of sufficient time to dedicate to developing and maintaining his skill. For that reason archers were drawn from amongst the sons of yeoman farmers and they expected, and received, high wages commensurate with their services.

Those services at their most basic level boiled down not to displaying individual feats of marksmanship, but upon laying down a heavy indirect fire upon the target; shooting rapidly into the air in order to create an arrow storm which dropped with considerable velocity on to the schiltrons from above, sowing death and dismay on the unarmoured men in the rear ranks rather than the better protected men in the front.

For the Scots then, winning battles meant attacking, marching forward and then maintaining the momentum of the assault long enough to break the enemy formations in front, while conversely for the English it was all too often a matter of simply standing their ground and shooting down enough Scots to stop them.

# Stirling Bridge and Falkirk

On a dark and stormy night in 1286 King Alexander III of Scotland plunged over a cliff, leaving no obvious heir beyond a grand-daughter who would herself die in 1290 before ascending the throne. In fact it eventually transpired that there were no fewer than thirteen 'Competitors' for the vacant throne, but the two with the strongest claim were John Balliol and Robert de Brus, Lord of Annandale. Both were descended from a younger brother of King William the Lion – David, Lord of the Garioch – and as they mustered their supporters and the prospect of civil war grew closer the question was submitted to King Edward I of England for arbitration.

On 17 November 1292 he eventually pronounced in favour of Balliol, but although Balliol was now King John I of Scotland, he also owed Edward knight service in respect of his considerable landholdings in England. Of itself this was a far from unusual state of affairs, indeed David of Garioch had also been Earl of Huntingdon. But, in June 1291, the Competitors had formally bound themselves to accept Edward's judgement by setting their seals to documents acknowledging his 'sovereign lordship of the kingdom of Scotland', and thereby his right to determine the succession.

Consequently, Edward now took the view that Balliol's vassalage was absolute and in 1293 he required knight service of Balliol and eighteen other lords in respect of their Scots lands for a war against France. Unsurprisingly this met with a point-blank refusal, although its impact was initially blunted by a similar refusal on the part of some of Edward's English lords. However early in 1296 King John formally renounced his vassalage.

Faced by this unacceptable challenge to his feudal authority, Edward marched north and stormed Berwick on 29 March. A part of his army led by John de Warenne, Earl of Surrey, then proceeded to lay siege to Dunbar and when the Scots, led by John Comyn (or Cumming), Earl of Buchan, counter-attacked they were disastrously defeated outside the town on 27 April. Pinned against the steep slope of Spott Dod, no fewer than 171 earls, knights and squires were captured and the brief battle effectively broke the back of Scots resistance. King John surrendered himself to Edward at Brechin on 10 July and shortly

## WILLIAM WALLACE

Wallace (c.1272-1305) is a surprisingly obscure figure, once the accumulated legend and downright invention is stripped away. It is however believed that he was a descendant of a Richard Wallace who came to Scotland in the 1130s in the service of Walter Fitzalan, the Steward. A seal which can be linked to Wallace on the 'Lubeck letter' of 1296 shows a hand drawing an arrow on a bow [WILELM]VS FILIVS ALANI WALAIS : 'William Son of Alan Wallace'] and although he is traditionally associated with Elderslie in Renfrewshire, this may point instead to his being a son of the Alan Wallace, a Crown tenant of lands in Ayrshire, who appended his seal to the 'Ragman Roll'. Much of the mystery surrounding Wallace centres around his sudden transition from total obscurity to prominence as one of the Guardians of Scotland; in reality he may have been a much less significant figure at the time whose importance was exaggerated by his Stewart and Bruce overlords in order to obscure the role played by Andrew de Moray and the Comyns.

afterwards Edward summoned all the land-holders of Scotland to formally acknowledge his overlordship once and for all. To all appearances Scotland had ceased to exist as an independent country, and its government was effectively entrusted to a bureaucrat named Hugh de Cressingham. Within months he was facing a widespread uprising.

William Wallace is of course the man most closely associated with the uprising, but surprisingly little is known of him until he 'raised his head' in May of 1297, stormed into Lanark and killed the English sheriff of Clydesdale, William Hesilrige. This may have been an isolated incident, but was more likely connected with a more general uprising in the south-west led by his father's feudal superior, James Stewart. Unfortunately this particular revolt collapsed in July, when Stewart literally backed himself into a corner and surrendered at Irvine, while Wallace fled to the Ettrick Forest.

Simultaneously however, or perhaps even a little earlier, a much more serious rebellion had broken out in the north of Scotland led by Andrew de Moray, a nephew of Sir John Comyn the younger, of Badenoch, otherwise known as The Red Comyn. Like his father, Sir Andrew de Moray, the Justiciar of Scotia (Scotland north of the Forth), he had been captured at Dunbar, but he escaped from imprisonment in Chester Castle sometime early in 1297 and by May was in the Black Isle raising his father's men. Whether he was doing so on his own initiative, or clandestinely acting as a proxy for his uncle in concert with the southern rebels, is perhaps a moot point. At any rate, enlisting the aid of an Inverness burgess named Andrew Pilche he began by ambushing William de Warine at Dunain, just outside Urquhart Castle on 25 May. An attack on the castle itself was beaten off next day, but Moray soon became unstoppable and by late summer not only had Urquhart been starved into submission, but Inverness, Elgin, Banff and Aberdeen were also in his hands.

On 11 June both the Earl of Buchan and his kinsman, Sir John Comyn of Badenoch were released and instructed by Edward to deal with him as an alternative to fighting in Gascony. However having returned home the pair blithely and quite unconvincingly professed their inability to catch up with, let alone defeat, the rebels.

Despite his preoccupation with the war in Gascony, Edward therefore ordered more troops to Scotland and, by the end of July, Cressingham was assembling an army of some 10,000 men at Roxburgh and only awaited the arrival of Edward's military commander, the Earl of Surrey, before moving north. In the face of this threatening concentration Wallace abandoned his base in Ettrick Forest and moved north to rendezvous with Moray outside Dundee at the beginning of September. Whilst it is common to credit Wallace with the victory at Stirling Bridge, Moray had the greater number of men and was the leader of a successful uprising. Wallace only became prominent after the battle and in later years became credited with a great many of Moray's achievements. In all the documents jointly sealed by the two men, Moray took precedence. Wallace now accompanied Moray as he marched on Stirling, traditionally regarded as the key to Scotland.

Surrey arrived there first, but only just. He was certainly there by 9 September, if not a day or two earlier, only to find Moray ensconced on the Abbey Craig, to the north east. This was bad news, for between the high rock of Stirling Castle and the rather higher rock of the Abbey Craig – facing each other almost exactly two kilometres apart – was a flat expanse of carseland on either side of the winding River Forth. The only practical way for an army to cross this area was by means of a long straight causeway – and Stirling Bridge.

Neither army was particularly large. Cressingham, we know, reported that he had assembled 10,000 foot (infantry) and 300 horse (cavalry) at Roxburgh in July, and these were subsequently joined by Surrey's own retinue which probably added at least another 50-100 horse. So far so good, but in the first place the figure of 10,000 foot is a suspiciously round one which was obviously intended to impress the King with Cressingham's diligence and zeal. The true figure may have been significantly lower. In any case medieval armies habitually suffered an alarming rate of wastage due to straggling, desertion and disease. Out of a comparable 9,093 troops mustered outside Caerlaverock exactly three years later, only 5,150 remained a month later. Admittedly, some of them must have been lost in besieging the castle and others in winning an easy victory on the River Cree, but notwithstanding it is an extraordinary decline. Applying, with reservations, a similar rate of attrition to Surrey and Cressingham's host would suggest there were probably little more than 6,000 foot and 300 horse at Stirling in early September 1297.

There is no comparable contemporary baseline for estimating the size of the Scots army, though there is no reason to suppose that it was not dissimilar. Despite the pre-eminent role accorded to Wallace by later chroniclers there can be little doubt that the greater number of them were Moray's men, raised in the sheriffdoms north of the Forth, which in later years fairly consistently produced levies of around 4-5,000 men. If Wallace's partisans added another 1,000 at the outside, that could have given them parity in numbers with Surrey and Cressingham's infantry. There were also some cavalry of course – a very manageable 180 according to a well-informed contemporary English chronicler, Walter of Guisborough.

Whatever their true number there were certainly enough Scots drawn up in their schiltrons below the Abbey Craig on the morning of 11 September 1297 to give Surrey pause to think. Thus far the Scots had obligingly caved in when confronted in the open field and in the hope that they might do so again he first sent James Stewart and then two Dominican friars to seek their submission. Neither embassy was successful and according to Guisborough, Wallace responded to the friars that 'We are not here to make peace but to do battle to defend ourselves and liberate our kingdom. Let them come on and we shall prove this to their very beards'.

Understandably enough, Surrey was more than a touch hesitant to come on and summoned a council of war at which a knight named Richard Lundie summed up his dilemma:

My lords if we cross the bridge we are dead men. For we can only go over two and two and the enemy are already formed up; their whole army can charge down upon us whenever they will.

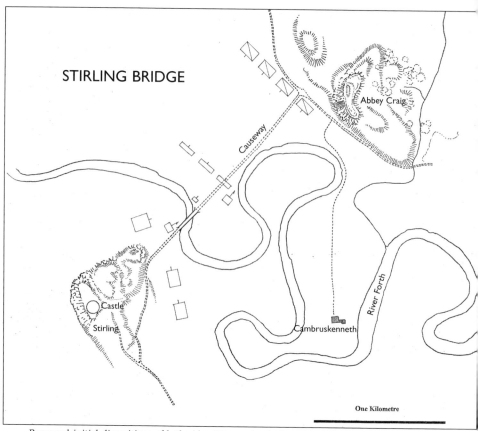

STIRLING BRIDGE

Abbey Craig

Causeway

River Forth

Castle

Stirling

Cambruskenneth

One Kilometre

*Presumed initial dispositions of both sides. The precise deployment of the four Scottish divisions is unknown and it is possible that they may have taken up a shallower but broader front. There is no indication at all as to the position of the small Scots cavalry contingent.*

Lundie proposed instead to lead a part of the army upstream, cross by one or other of the fords and so come in on the Scots' flank, but this was flatly rejected by Cressingham. The hostile Guisborough alleges this was because he considered it likely the Scots would simply withdraw, thus prolonging the campaign and its expense. A more viable objection to Lundie's cunning plan might be that it is usually accounted a mistake to divide a force in the face of the enemy and that the Scots might overwhelm the flanking division before sufficient of the main body could get across the bridge. Be that as it may the upshot was that Surrey supported Cressingham and ordered a frontal attack straight across the narrow wooden bridge.

It was of course just what Moray had been hoping for and as Guisborough complained:

> Thus, amazing though it is to relate and terrible as was to be its outcome, all these experienced men, though they knew the enemy was at hand, began to cross a bridge so narrow that even two horsemen could scarcely and with much difficulty ride side by side and so they did all morning, without let or hindrance, until the vanguard was on one side of the river and the remainder of the army on the other.

Wallace Monument

One of the original bridge piers exposed

*A combination of low tide and the long dry summer of 2003 exposes one of the original bridge piers, just a few metres upstream from its fifteenth century replacement.*

*The fifteenth-century stone bridge which replaced the original and carried most armies across the Forth thereafter.*

It was at this point, presumably around noon, that Moray attacked. We know nothing as to how his men were deployed other than that they formed a line of schiltrons. Most mediaeval armies were grouped into three 'battles' or divisions, but for some reason the Scots normally favoured four. Each division will in turn have been comprised of two or three individual schiltrons, each about 500 strong and drawn up six-ranks deep.

Cressingham, commanding the English vanguard was obviously heavily outnumbered from the outset, for it appears he had only 150 horse under Sir Marmaduke de Thweng, 1800 billmen and archers, and fifty crossbowmen from the Stirling Castle garrison, under Sir Richard Waldegrave. Of itself this was bad enough, but the full horror of his situation can only be appreciated by a glance at the map.

His primary responsibility was to cover the northern end of the bridge, but presumably he had to take up a position sufficiently forward from it to allow the rest of the army to cross behind him. Since the river downstream of the bridge loops back on itself to almost lap against the eastern side of the causeway, all of the Scots must have been deployed to the west of the causeway, guiding their left flank off it as they advanced. Then, as they came into contact with Cressingham's men, their great superiority in numbers allowed them to wheel around, caving in the English left flank and driving them past the bridge-end and into the cul-de-sac formed by the loop of the river.

What followed was more of a massacre than a battle. With their backs to the river the English began panicking. Sir Marmaduke de Thweng managed to cut his way back to the bridge and escape with some of his men. Some 300 of the billmen and archers managed to swim to safety, but with Surrey and the rest of the army watching helplessly from the other side of the river, the vanguard was quite literally wiped out. There is no evidence that any prisoners were taken and Cressingham's corpse was widely reported to have been flayed.

Entrusting Stirling Castle to William de Warine (the former governor of Urquhart) and Sir Marmaduke de Thweng, Surrey fled, abandoning the rest of his army to its fate. The Scots caught up with it on the carselands to the south-east of Stirling, where Bruce would win his great victory nearly twenty years later, capturing the baggage train and then harrying the survivors all the way to Berwick. It was, by any standards, a complete victory, but unlike Bannockburn it was far from being decisive.

With one exception the Scots casualties are unknown, but the loss of that one man was to have serious and far-reaching repercussions, for it was Andrew de Moray. The Scots chronicler Fordun simply says that he 'fell wounded', but he was dead by November and his loss would be keenly felt. During the rest of the year and over the winter which followed, English discomfiture was increased by a series of destructive Scots raids as far south as Durham. At some point Wallace was formally appointed 'Guardian of the kingdom of Scotland and commander of its army', in the name of the absent King John, but already Edward I was assembling another army.

Still pre-occupied by the French war he only returned to England on 14 March

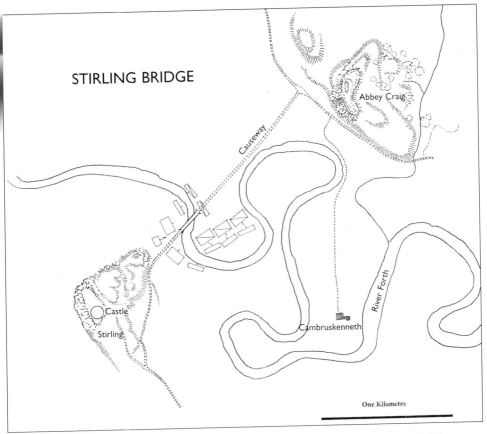

STIRLING BRIDGE

Abbey Craig

Causeway

River Forth

Castle

Stirling

Cambruskenneth

One Kilometre

*The Scots schiltrons have outflanked and crushed the English left, cutting the advance guard off from the bridge and driving it into the cul-de-sac formed by the river bend.*

1298 and it was not until 25 June that his forces were concentrated at Roxburgh. The still extant rolls show a total of 214 knights and 900 troopers in the King's pay at Falkirk, together with another 1,000 cavalry serving in the feudal retinues of the Earls. The infantry on the other hand are rather more problematic. There were certainly a total of about 500 mercenary crossbowmen, and these should have been supplemented by 2,000 archers and billmen levied out of Lancashire and Cheshire, and 10,500 from Wales, although the numbers present will have been very much less. Only half of those summoned for the Caerlaverock campaign actually appeared and this proportion was by no means unusual. It is entirely possible therefore that Edward had no more than 8,000 infantry and perhaps even less by the time he reached Falkirk, for the campaign got off to a bad start.

Leaving Roxburgh on 3 July Edward followed the traditional invasion route northwards along Lauderdale, by way of Soutra, to reach Kirkliston, just to the west of Edinburgh two weeks later. There he halted. It had been his intention to resupply his army through the small ports scattered along the south shore of the Firth of Forth, but bad weather delayed the convoy and the surrounding countryside had already been devastated by the Scots themselves. Not until 20 July was he ready to move forward again and in the meantime the Welsh had turned mutinous. To make matters worse he had no idea where the Scots army might be and was beginning to suspect that it may have slipped past him to raid into England again, but no sooner had he determined to retreat to Edinburgh to rest and resupply than the situation changed dramatically.

The Scots were, as it happened very close at hand, in the Torwood, near Falkirk and when told that they intended to harass his retreat, the King snarled that he 'would not trouble them to seek me' and set his army in motion at once. The night of 21 July was spent outside Linlithgow and next morning he came up with the Scots army at first light, just to the south of Falkirk.

There is an excellent account of the battle by Walter of Guisborough which provides a reasonably detailed and convincing picture of how it was fought, but nevertheless there are two major problems with Falkirk. The first concerns the site of the battle. Guisborough states only that the Scots had taken up a position 'on hard ground and on one side of a hillock, next to Falkirk', although the Scalachronica written by Sir Thomas Gray, does at least say that it was 'on this side of Falkirk', which narrows the field somewhat. Since Edward was approaching from Linlithgow, the current consensus amongst historians is that Wallace had deployed his men on the southern slope of the hillside below Callendar Wood, with the boggy valley of the Glen Burn to his front. There is however a major objection to this site in that it requires Wallace to have drawn his army up at right angles to the English line of approach from Linlithgow, in a very constricted space with his back to a wood and no real line of retreat. Conversely this location in turn requires Edward to leave the Roman road and make a rather improbable swing far to the south across some very broken terrain in order to come at Wallace head on.

In all the circumstances therefore a far more convincing location would be up on the burgh muir of Falkirk where the later battle would be fought in 1746. One English account certainly speaks of the battle being fought on 'the plain which is called Falkirk', which would support this interpretation, as would the fact that it is indeed 'next to Falkirk'.

According to Guisborough, the Scots were massed in four great circles of spearmen, with bodies of archers set between, and 'at the back, on the extreme flank, were their knights' – some 500 cavalry, commanded by James Stewart. Although clear enough in itself, this description leads to the second problem with the battle – the Scots army.

Supposedly the complete expulsion of the English after Stirling Bridge permitted the Scots to re-establish their civil administration. Indeed even before the battle Cressingham had warned that 'in some shires the Scots have appointed and established bailiffs and officials', while afterwards the Scots themselves advertised that Scotland 'was now recovered by war from the power of the English' and invited the resumption of trading links with the Continent. As Guardian, Wallace should therefore have been able to raise a proper army to face the anticipated English invasion by summoning out the men of each sheriffdom and mustering them for training at a central point such as Stirling. Instead he

*The Wallace monument
on the Abbey Craig.*

*A remarkable sculpture depicting the Australian actor Mel Gibson as William Wallace.*

seems once again to have spent the spring and early summer in his old refuge of Ettrick Forest and the army which he led to disaster at Falkirk was an untrained rabble.

Once again, while there are no reliable figures available on their numbers, it is possible to arrive at a reasonably convincing estimate. It is clear from the known casualties – Sir John Stewart of Jedburgh; Andrew Moray of Bothwell; James Graham of Abercorn; Sir John Graham (buried with Stewart in Falkirk kirkyard); and MacDuff of Fife – that the Comyns and their northern levies were absent. Guisborough also states the Robert Bruce, the Earl of Carrick and future king 'held Ayr and the West', instead of fighting at Falkirk and this is obliquely confirmed by Walter Bower's Scotichronicon which blames him for the defeat.

Exclusive of the western sheriffdoms, whose men will have been with Bruce, the southern and central ones were reckoned in 1650 to be capable of levying some 8,300 infantrymen between them – then as in 1298 the cavalry were assessed separately. Although these figures obviously date from 350 years after Falkirk the basic demographics are unlikely to have changed by very much and at the very least they provide us with an absolute upper limit for Wallace's infantry. It would certainly be prudent however to reduce those numbers by a third, first to allow for an admittedly erratic population growth, and secondly for the optimistic nature of the assessments in the first place. This then equates to an estimated total of about 5,500 infantry actually present on the field and confirmation that this figure may just about be right can be found by analysing the contributions of the individual sheriffdoms.

MacDuff's large sheriffdom of Fife and Kinross should have been capable of producing an adjusted figure of 1200 fencibles in 1298, as should the combined sheriffdoms of Midlothian and Haddington, while the central sheriffdoms of Stirling, Linlithgow and Lanark could have produced a similar combined total of 1300 men. The Merse and Teviotdale on the other hand might theoretically have been capable of mustering 1800 infantry, though in 1298 that figure will have been substantially reduced by the English hold on Roxburgh. The essential point therefore is that these four sets of figures directly translate into the four schiltrons of pikemen, each about 1,000 strong, with the remainder being the archers under Sir John Stewart of Jedburgh.

Had Robert Bruce been present after all, the levies from the three sheriffdoms of Dumfries; Wigton and Kirkcudbright, and Ayr and Renfrew could have added, by the same calculation, another 2,400 men. This alone is sufficient to explain Bower's complaint. Had Bruce not been so reluctant to fight under King John's banner, the strength of Wallace's army at Falkirk would have been increased by fifty per cent – a significant factor by any standards and certainly sufficient to have given him parity with Edward's infantry.

A third problem however, and one glossed over since the days of 'Blind Harry', is that while unquestionably a good partisan leader, William Wallace's military abilities were simply not up to the job of organising, training and leading a conventional military force.

This is starkly apparent from what followed. While Moray had not only used his schiltrons offensively at Stirling Bridge, but actually manoeuvred with them, swinging them round in that great wheel which crushed Cressingham's left wing, Wallace by contrast simply drew up his army in an open field and froze. He may perhaps have been acutely aware that his men were insufficiently trained to do anything more than stand their ground, which is why he may have drawn them up in the four great circles in the first place. But his famous exhortation recorded in the contemporary Chronicle of Rishanger that 'I have browghte yowe to the ryng, hoppe yef ye canne!' all too eloquently reveals a commander completely out of his depth. All he could do was array his men and await the outcome.

Having brought the Scots to bay after a forced march, Edward was in no hurry to act precipitately. He proposed to halt, pitch tents and feed both men and horses – who had eaten nothing since the previous afternoon – while his infantry closed up. His cavalry commanders on the other hand, thinking perhaps of what had happened at Stirling, successfully urged an immediate attack.

The English cavalry were organised in four brigades, an unusual arrangement, probably in order that each brigade should take on one of the schiltrons, and also appear to have intended attacking in echelon rather than line abreast. This may be inferred from the fact that the vanguard, led by the Earl of Lincoln, moved forward first – and almost immediately got bogged down in a very marshy area, perhaps in the valley of the Glen Burn. Eventually Lincoln got across by moving to his left, but by so doing he moved across the front of the other advancing brigades and so reversed the echelon.

The next brigade, led by Anthony Bek, the Bishop of Durham, instead of coming up on Lincoln's left, swung around the bog to his right and, intentionally, or otherwise, ended up on the Scots' left flank. In the process the 400 strong brigade had become separated from the much stronger King's brigade following behind, and Bek decided to delay his attack until it came up. However at about this time Lincoln, supported by the fourth brigade under Surrey, finally got into action, charging and routing the Scots cavalry and Bek's knights, contrary to his orders, immediately charged forward as well, followed in their turn by the King's brigade.

At first the English cavalry did well. Not only were the Scots cavalry driven from the field in that first rush – which would also argue against the Callendar Wood position – but the archers posted between the schiltrons were ridden down as well, and their commander, Sir John Stewart, killed.

Nevertheless the schiltrons themselves held firm. According to Edward's horse lists 111 animals were killed as his cavalry vainly tried to break in, which speaks for a certain determination on the part of the riders, but the collapse of Wallace's position was, as it always had been, just a matter of time.

Once Edward's infantry came up, his cavalry fell back to regroup while an arrow storm was unleashed on the schiltrons. Unable to move, they soon began to fall apart under the deadly hail and then broke in the face of a renewed attack by the English cavalry, supported this time by billmen. Biblical numbers of the Scots, according to the English chroniclers, were slain; ranging from 10,000 all the way up to 60,000, which considering that Wallace probably had as few as 5-6,000 men on the field, is remarkable. There is no doubting that significant casualties were inflicted by the archers and that once they broke in upon the shattered schiltrons, the English cavalry will also have done considerable damage before the Scots reached the woodlands immediately to the west of the battlefield. On the other hand, if they had been posted immediately in front of Callendar Wood it would have covered their retreat at the very outset.

Wallace's army may have been scattered rather than destroyed and although Edward had undoubtedly won the battle, he gained very little from it. Stirling was re-occupied and acted as his headquarters for the next two weeks while raiding parties ranged as far as Perth and St. Andrews. But he still had trouble keeping his army supplied and after some of the feudal contingents returned home, he had no alternative but to withdraw and, after a punitive raid into Ayrshire, was back in Carlisle by 9 September.

Towards the end of the year Robert Bruce, the Earl of Carrick, and Sir John Comyn, the younger, of Badenoch were elected as joint Guardians, in place of Wallace. Had they been able to act together they might have made an effective combination, but while the Comyns remained loyal to their kinsman, John Balliol, Bruce was intent on reviving his grandfather's claim to the throne and somehow contrived, as at Falkirk, to be elsewhere when most needed.

Thus when Edward invaded again in the summer of 1300 it was Badenoch and his cousin, the Earl of Buchan, who were defeated in a battle on the river Cree in Dumfriesshire. Further English incursions were made into southern Scotland each year thereafter, and although the Scots were no longer prepared to meet the English in open battle, they constantly harassed and skirmished with the invaders. Then Edward settled the business by marching northwards into the Comyn heartlands in Buchan and Moray in 1304, which at last forced Badenoch to sue for peace. Thoroughly weary of the war, Edward granted most of the 'rebels' generous terms, including freedom from forfeiture of their lands, but for William Wallace there was to be no mercy. Captured the following year, he was executed in London, but within months a fresh uprising had broken out in Scotland, this time led by Robert Bruce, Earl of Carrick.

# *Bannockburn*

T he road to Bannockburn began not with yet another uprising against English rule, but with a murder and bloody civil war in Scotland. Despite the later fame accorded to William Wallace, resistance to Edward I before 1304 had very largely been sustained by the Comyns, in the name of their kinsman King John. In the face of that avowed support for his rival, Robert Bruce, the grandson of the old Competitor had co-operated less than wholeheartedly in the struggle for independence and surrendered to Edward as early as 1302. To be sure, he and Balliol's nephew, the Red Comyn (Sir John Comyn of Badenoch) jointly served together as Guardians. Theirs was an uneasy relationship which ended dramatically on 10 February 1306 with Badenoch stabbed to death in the kirk of the

Grey Friars in Dumfries and Bruce an excommunicate fugitive. Thus far Bruce's behaviour had been extremely circumspect and may in some degree have been guided by an unlikely hope that one day Edward might reverse his fateful decision and award the Scots crown to the lords of Annandale. Now, with nothing left to lose, Bruce rode hard for Perth and at Scone, just two weeks later, had himself crowned Robert I, King of Scots. There was to be no turning back.

Fighting against the Comyns and their MacDougall allies on the one hand, and the English on the other, Bruce fared badly at first. He and his men were surprised and scattered by Aymer de Valence, Earl of Pembroke, at Methven outside Perth on 19 June 1306. Not only was he reduced to a hunted fugitive – 'King Bob' – but there were precious few places for him to go, for the Highlands were effectively closed to him by the Comyns and MacDougalls. In the end he found refuge on Rathlin Island, off the Antrim coast, under the protection of the MacDougalls' rivals, the MacDonalds of the Isles.

In February of the following year two of his brothers, Alexander and Thomas, returned to the mainland only to be ambushed in the Galloway Hills by John MacDougall of Lorne, and hanged at Carlisle. Undaunted, (if not inspired by that famous spider) Bruce followed in March, coming ashore this time in Ayrshire at Turnberry Castle and disappearing into his own hills before Lorne could catch him. At Glen Trool in April he succesfully ambushed an English column by rolling boulders down on them and at Loudon Hill defeated another detachment in something approaching a stand-up fight. Consequently Edward I resolved to return to Scotland himself to deal with the 'rebels', only to die at Burgh-by-Sands on the Solway coast on 7 July.

This was the turning point. While the succession to the English throne was undisputed, Edward II needed time to establish himself as king, and that meant that Scotland was a much lower priority. This in turn left Bruce free to concentrate on winning the civil war. Moving north he first harried the MacDougall lands in Argyll with the aid of the MacDonalds, then forced John of Lorne to accept a truce while he passed up the Great Glen and into the Comyn heartlands of Moray and the North-East. The forces ranged against him there appeared formidable, but Badenoch was dead and the Earl of Buchan had never been much of a soldier. One by one the castles fell and, despite falling seriously ill during the winter, Bruce won a decisive victory over the Comyns at Barra, just outside Inverurie, on 23 May 1308. The herschip or harrying of Buchan

| ROBERT BRUCE |
| --- |

Robert de Brus, or Bruce (1273-1329), is more properly Robert I, King of Scots, but is best known to history simply as The Bruce, and well deserves his reputation as 'the Hero King'. Whilst his most important achievement in the longer term was probably in first restoring unity to a Scotland split by rival factions, albeit at the point of his sword, ultimately he was a more successful general than a politician. When considering him simply as a military leader, it is apparent that he belongs in the top class, for he was one of those unusual commanders who could switch with ease from guerrilla warfare to fight and win a conventional battle. There were no special or unusual factors affecting the outcome of the battle of Bannockburn, which could have been fought anywhere in Western Europe with the same result. It was won simply because Bruce outmanoeuvred and then crushed his opponent in open battle.

*The famous Pilkington Jackson statue of Bruce at Bannockburn.*

followed and by the end of the year all of the castles north of the river Tay, except Banff, were in Bruce's hands and the civil war was all but over – a point heavily underlined by his convening his first parliament at St. Andrews in March 1309.

Edward II came north in the following year but Bruce declined to meet him in battle and nothing was achieved. On the contrary, by 1312 Bruce was sufficiently confident to raid into northern England and by March 1314 Stirling was the only fortress of any importance still in English hands. Although the castle itself was secure, the governor, Sir Philip de Moubray, was all-too aware of his isolation and agreed that if Stirling was not relieved by Midsummer Day 1314, he would surrender. So both sides prepared for the climactic battle.

For Edward II the matter was straightforward enough. So long as he had Stirling, he still had his hands around Scotland's throat. There was therefore no question but that he should march northwards to save the castle. Bruce's position is less straightforward but when stripped to its essentials, clear enough. According to John Barbour, when Edward Bruce informed his brother of the agreement, the King was unhappy at the prospect of having to face an English expeditionary force in something like a conventional battle, but it is hard to see that it committed him to anything of the sort. Quite the contrary, for the truce and the undertaking to surrender on a given date meant that the Scots army was not immobilised in siege lines around the place. Bruce was completely free to choose whether to avoid combat and simply harry the invaders until they withdrew, as he had done so often before, or to stand and fight on ground of his own choosing. The time had come to fight, and the fact that he deliberately and with malice aforethought chose to take his stand at Bannockburn shows he knew exactly what he was doing. He intended from the outset to fight. Bannockburn was a trap and Stirling merely the bait.

Most of the documentation that could have provided an accurate picture of the size of the English army assembled at Wark that summer was lost after the battle, but the *Vita Edwardi Secundi* gives him a little over 2,000 cavalry. In March Edward also summoned no fewer than 21,540 infantry, but surviving correspondence indicates more than the usual reluctance on the part of the county authorities to produce them. Taking past experience into account would suggest that only something like 10,000 actually turned up – and even that number will have been reduced by the time they actually reached Bannockburn.

Be that as it may Edward crossed the border on 17 June, following the traditional invasion route north up Lauderdale to Soutra and then down to Edinburgh, where he halted for two days in order to let the tail end of his column close up and for supplies to be landed at Leith. By the evening of 22 June his cavalry were at Falkirk, just ten miles short of their objective. Perhaps unduly conscious of the fact that only two days remained until the deadline Edward was pushing hard and once again the infantry were straggling. Up until this point the greater part of the Scots army had been encamped in the Torwood, but now they withdrew to their pre-prepared fighting positions athwart the Roman road to Stirling where it crossed a marshy stream called the Bannockburn.

The size, and to some extent the organisation of the Scots army is uncertain, but Barbour, who provides the only substantial Scots account explicitly states there

MacDonald of the Isles as depicted by the Victorian artist McIan.

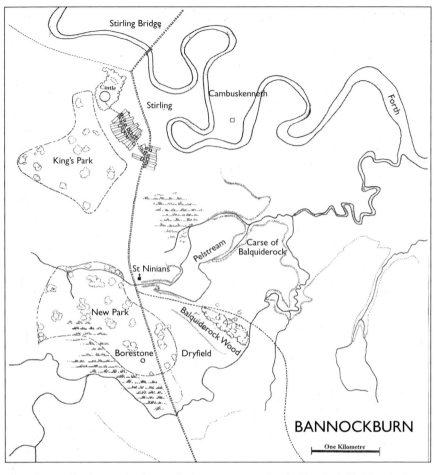

*General map of battle area. On day one the Scots were occupying the New Park, blocking the Roman Road. The greater part of the English army therefore approached along the bridle track known as The Way. A reconnaissance party led by Clifford attempted to find a direct route off the Carse over the Pelstream but was intercepted and turned back by Moray's men attacking downhill from St Ninians.*

were 'four bataillis ordaynit' including the King's. Some historians, relying on English accounts describing the initial onset, have argued there were only three divisions, and that the fourth division commanded by Walter Stewart was merely an invention by Barbour to flatter his son, King Robert II. Barbour's narrative however is persuasive, makes sense – particularly in commenting that young Stewart had the more experienced Douglas as a minder – and is internally cohesive when he comes to describe the battle. Moreover, the fact remains that Scots medieval armies did ordinarily form in four divisions rather than the three customary elsewhere.

It also has to be stressed that notwithstanding statements in many secondary sources there is absolutely no evidence at all as to the geographical composition of three front-line divisions or 'bataillis', commanded by the Earl of Moray, Sir

Edward Bruce and young Walter Stewart respectively. Only the fourth division commanded by the King himself is described by Barbour in any detail. It apparently comprised 'The men of Carrik halely; And of Arghile, and of Kentyr; And off the Illes, quhar off wes Syr Anguss of the Ile and. But, all thai; He of the plane land had alsua; Off arymt men a mekill rout'.

In other words it was made up of Highland clansmen from Argyll, Kintyre and the Western Isles under Angus Og MacDonald, some of his old followers from Carrick in the south-west and a large contingent from the 'plane land' – presumably the central lowlands.

As to the other divisions; while it would be tempting to suggest that Moray's men were drawn from his recently acquired earldom, Barbour states that 'to maynteyme his baner; Lordis, that of gret worschip wer; War assygnyt with thair mengne; In till his bataill for to be' which clearly indicates it was a composite formation made up of various contingents. Stewart's division may well have been made up of those men from his native south west who had not already been claimed for the King's one, but there is nothing at all to say who might have served under Edward Bruce.

It is, however, possible to establish the approximate size of the divisions. Advancing in a single line during the second day's fighting the first three spanned the entrance to the Carse of Balquiderock, which happens to be exactly one kilometre wide. Allowing one metre of frontage for each man in the first of the six ranks would indicate a maximum of 6,000 men, or say 2,000 in each division. In practice making allowance for the very necessary gaps between the divisions and the individual schiltrons when on the move will reduce this figure to a more manageable 1,500 pikemen apiece, although this does not include the archers grouped in front and behind. Allowing a similar number to the King's division therefore points to the Scots having something like 5-6,000 pikemen at Bannockburn, perhaps 1-2,000 archers, and, according to Barbour, some 500 cavalry.

Unlike Wallace's rabble at Falkirk sixteen years before, Bruce's pikemen were sufficiently well trained to be able to move and manoeuvre on the battlefield. In addition there is the matter of the so-called 'small folk', who according to legend, or at least to Barbour,

*An almost exactly contemporary illustration from the Carlisle charter of Scots attacking the city in 1315. Note how they are easily distinguished from the English defenders by the wearing of hooded cloaks and what appear to be bare legs.*

were a motley rabble of camp-followers who turned up to watch the proceedings and managed to get mistaken for Scots reinforcements by the embattled English.

An immediate flaw in this interpretation is that the Scots baggage train was not behind the fighting line at all, but had instead been sent across the river to Cambuskenneth Abbey – where ironically enough it was attacked and plundered by the renegade earl of Atholl. Instead the 'small folk' were almost certainly secondary levies, called out only after the English crossed the border and neither sufficiently trained nor equipped to stand in the main battle-line. Barbour indeed earlier used exactly the same term 'small folk' to describe the Earl of Buchan's raw levies at the battle of Barra in 1308.

An appreciation of the terrain is absolutely essential to understanding how the battle was fought. Edward was approaching Stirling along the old Roman road from Falkirk, which crossed the Bannockburn by a ford at Milton and then continued northwards along a spine of high ground, past St Ninians to Stirling and on of course to Stirling Bridge. Between Milton and St Ninians much of this high ground was wooded and largely enclosed as a Royal hunting preserve. This was the New Park (so-called to distinguish it from the older King's Park beneath Stirling Castle), and progress along this less than inviting stretch of road was supposedly discouraged by the digging of a belt of 'pottes', or pits set with wooden stakes on either side, at Milton.

Further to the west the land on either side of the Bannockburn became progressively marshier and the country beyond more broken, discouraging any large scale troop movements in that direction. To the east however there was a well-used bridle path, referred to simply as 'The Way' that had largely come about as a result of local traffic being diverted away from the New Park. This crossed the Bannockburn nearly two kilometres downstream from Milton and skirted along the northern edge of Balquiderock Wood before climbing to join the Roman road at St Ninians. During the battle it also provided Edward's troops with an easy access route on to the Carse, or more properly the Carse of Balquiderock, a roughly

*The battlefield of Bannockburn: the Carse of Balquiderock looking towards where the Scots army emerged from Balquiderock Wood. The Bannockburn itself is just off to the left of the panorama. The distant houses right of centre are in the Broomridge area where Moray and Clifford clashed on the first day. The slight elevation to the right, now crowned with trees, will have been an obvious place for Edward II to position himself.*

Scots Army just in front of the woods

triangular area bounded on two sides by the Bannockburn and the Pelstream Burn, and on the third by Balquiderock Wood.

The Carse of Balquiderock is a flat area of silty clay, sometimes speckled with shallow pools of standing water, but on the whole firmer and much drier than the lower and boggier peat carselands to the north and east. At first sight it provided an excellent camping ground for Edward and his army, particularly since the pools provided the large quantities of fresh water required by his numerous cavalry. Unfortunately it suffered from the fatal defect that all three boundaries were significant military obstacles which severely restricted their ability to get in and out of it. This was particularly true of the Wood of Balquiderock which cloaks an abrupt fifteen metre (50-60 foot) rise from the Carse to a another flat area known as the Dryfield of Balquiderock. There have been suggestions in recent years that the main battle was fought on the Dryfield rather than the Carse but this cannot be sustained by any sensible reading either of the sources or of the ground itself, for it would require Edward's cavalry to climb up a considerable slope from their camp to this alternative battlefield and then to fight that battle with the wood (and that steep slope) at their backs.

On the morning of 23 June Bruce was in position in the New Park, with his own division covering the ford at Milton, his brother's and Stewart's behind in reserve, and Moray's back at St Ninians. This seemingly odd deployment has been interpreted as evidence that Bruce was still uncertain whether to fight or run, but the events of the day reveal no such ambiguity.

The first, and certainly the most famous clash, came late in the afternoon as the cavalry of the English vanguard, led by the Earls of Gloucester and Hereford, advanced along the Roman road towards the ford at Milton. At that point the Scots cavalry, who had been shadowing their approach, decided to break contact and run for home, whereupon some of the English cavalry spurred after them in pursuit only to find Bruce drawing his own division out of the trees. At the same time they may also have become uncomfortably aware of the existence of the 'pottes' and so drew up, although Hereford's nephew, Henry de Bohun, got too far ahead and was engaged in hand-to-hand fighting with Bruce himself.

According to the Scots, Bohun, seeing the King riding alone in front of his division attacked him with lance couched, but in one of Barbour's drier passages 'Schyr Henry myssit the nobill Kyng', who thereupon stood up in his stirrups and

bashed his head in with an axe. The Vita on the other hand says that Bohun, having ventured too far ahead of his companions, was trying to return when he was intercepted and killed. Either way, the Scots infantry then came forward and engaged the rest of the English vanguard. Edward Bruce's division also came out of the trees in support and the cavalry were rolled back across the Bannockburn in considerable disorder.

Dramatic though the clash might have seemed, both sides probably regarded it as a success. While Bruce must have been at least prepared to fight at the entry, his ostentatious appearance in what was clearly a very strong position was probably no more than a demonstration aimed at encouraging the English to avoid a frontal assault by slipping around his invitingly open left flank. Edward for his part, forewarned that the Scots were waiting for him in the New Park, had indeed already struck off along the Way in order to outflank the Scots position, covered by Hereford and Gloucester's probe. However once across the Bannockburn and on to the Carse of Balquiderock, Edward soon realised he was in a trap, for his real advance guard; a force of cavalry, led by Sir Robert Clifford, got as far as St Ninians, where the Way rejoined the Roman road, only to be intercepted by Moray's division, placed there by Bruce for that very purpose.

This fight was much more serious than the one by the Entry, but once Barbour's dramatic embellishments are stripped away, the outlines are straightforward enough. Skirting around the Balquiderock escarpment Clifford was in a fair way, as he thought, to cutting off the Scots' line of retreat, when a single schiltron, just 500 men, came out of the trees and rolled down the hill towards him. Why Moray chose to attack with just one of his three schiltrons is unclear. Barbour claims that he was caught unawares and that these men were all that he could lead up in time to stop Clifford, but while this is certainly possible, a more likely explanation is that the frontage available was severely restricted by the heavily wooded terrain. At any rate Clifford accepted the challenge and attacked, on a site traditionally marked by two standing stones at Newhouse, only to find like just about everybody else in military history that unsupported cavalry charges against resolute infantry tend to come to grief. Sir Thomas Gray was unhorsed, wounded and captured, while Sir William Deyncourt was killed along with his brother Reginald. Rather more horses were killed and after the first futile attempts to break into the Scottish formation, the knights were reduced to throwing axes, maces and lances at the Scots. In the end the matter was decided by the arrival of a second schiltron commanded by James Douglas and in the face of this threat, Clifford drew off and the fighting ended for the day.

Bruce now had the English penned up in a trap as he had surely planned all along. That night he redeployed his whole army in the Dryfield of Balquiderock and at dawn next morning, Monday, 24 June 1314, he led it down through the woods and out on to the Carse for a reprise of Moray's great victory seventeen years before.

As they came out of the tree-line the Scots knelt to pray – which had the practical advantage of giving time for the rear ranks to get out of the trees and form up (during the American Civil War it was established that it required fully half an

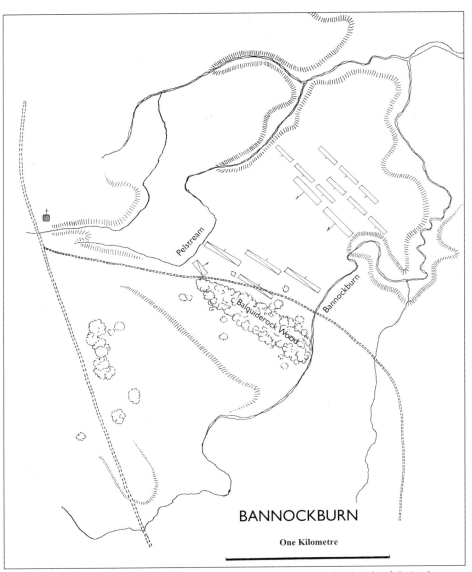

**BANNOCKBURN**

One Kilometre

*Presumed initial dispositions on second day – depicted rather more neatly for the sake of clarity than was probably the case.*

hour to reform the ranks of a division after passing through a wood). Then, to the astonishment and consternation of the English cavalry, instead of standing on the defensive, the Scots rolled forward in an all out attack.

According to Barbour the Scots' front line comprised three divisions drawn up in echelon, with Edward Bruce's men forward on the right, Moray's in the centre and Stewart's on the left, while the King's own division was in reserve behind the centre. How the English were drawn up is much less clear. Barbour for one

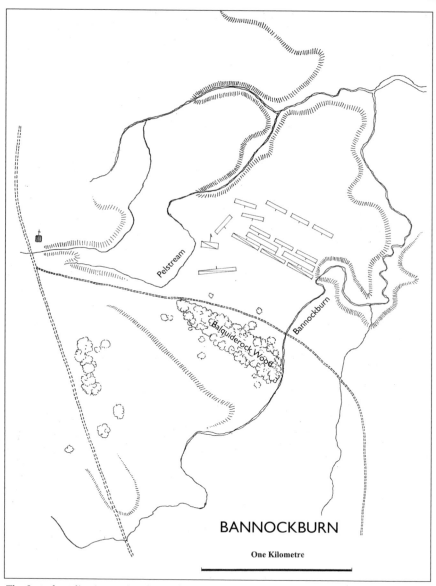

## BANNOCKBURN

**One Kilometre**

*The Scots front line is pressing the English cavalry back upon its supports, but in the process has contracted towards the right, allowing English archers to attack the now exposed left flank. This threat is neutralised first by the Scots cavalry and then by the reserve division under the King himself.*

contrasts the orderly deployment of the Scots with the way the English were jammed together in a solid mass. They had spent an uncomfortable night getting across the increasingly boggy Bannockburn and into the Carse, with no real certainty as to how they were going to get out of it again. Their dispositions were in consequence dictated by circumstances rather than choice, with all the cavalry out in front under the command of the Earl of Gloucester. Interestingly though the

Lanercost Chronicle adds that 'the English archers were thrown forward before the line and the Scottish archers engaged them, a few being killed and wounded on either side; but the King of England's archers put the others to flight'.

Since the fight was confined to the archers on both sides it may be concluded that this simply represented an exchange between the opposing picket lines and that the Scots, far from being put to flight, fell back in order to clear the front of the advancing pikemen. Having hastily mustered and mounted his cavalry, Gloucester immediately charged Edward Bruce's division, but getting too far ahead of his men was brought down and killed. One English account states that having gone in without waiting to put on his heraldic surcoat, he was unrecognised by the Scots who might otherwise have spared him for ransom.

Instead of passively forming a circle, Edward Bruce's men simply closed up, levelled their pikes and kept moving, being joined in turn by Moray's and Stewart's divisions as they came up until, as Barbour relates 'thar three bataillis wer, All syd besid, fechtand weill ner'. Already the English were in deep trouble for with their own infantry close behind, the cavalry were unable to turn away and disengage, yet horses find it very difficult to move backwards. For so long as the Scots maintained the momentum of their advance, slow though it may have been, the English disorganisation increased exponentially. This was also particularly marked in the dismal performance of the English archers, who were perforce blindly lofting their shafts over, and perhaps into their own cavalry. The Scots archers on the other hand could afford to shoot in a rather flatter arc in the sure and certain expectation of hitting something.

*A modern re-enactment of a Scots schiltron preparing to meet an English cavalry charge.*

*English cavalry closely backed up by infantry.*

After the initial clash a subtle but very significant change occurred to the Scottish front line as the pikemen closed up into a solid mass to push the English back. Edward Bruce was no doubt guiding his advance off the Bannockburn on his right flank and so the other divisions, the schiltrons within each division and the individual pikemen within each schiltron all gradually closed in to the right. At the same time the Carse widens a little once within its throat and so as the Scots battle-line contracted towards its right a substantial gap inevitably opened up between its left flank and the Pelstream.

It was this gap which at last gave some of the English archers an opportunity to wheel forward and shoot straight into the exposed flank of Stewart's division. There is no doubting from the Scots' accounts that this archery caused some serious damage, but it is less clear how they dealt with it. Barbour very graphically describes how the archers were ridden down by Scots cavalry commanded by Sir Robert Keith, and this is actually perfectly feasible if they were attached to the King's reserve division, close behind the front line, rather than back up on the Dryfield as shown in some reconstructions. They would thus have been well placed to respond very quickly to the threat, and with only a short distance to ride will have burst in upon the archers before they in turn could react – just as Barbour describes. Against this the various English accounts emphatically declare that all the Scots were on foot, and even on the Scots' side Hector Boece, writing in the early sixteenth century, related that it was pikemen, improbably led by Edward Bruce, who dealt with the archers. Tellingly he confirms that they 'come on thair bakkis', ie. took them in rear.

On balance however, given the brief and peripheral nature of the action, Barbour's version, seems likelier. In any case once the archers had been dealt with, Bruce swung his own reserve division into the gap in line with the others so that; 'all their for battailis with that wer; Fechtand in a front hardyly'. Having committed his immediate tactical reserve, Bruce now called forward his final one, the so-called 'small folk'. In Barbour's epic tale their appearance alone was sufficient to decide the struggle, for the English took them to be a second Scots army and thereupon threw down their arms and fled. Similar things have indeed happened in battles, but while it is a pity to spoil a good story, none of the English accounts say anything of the sort – which is not to prevent the Scots themselves from assuming that the arrival of the 'small folk' and the English collapse were connected.

At any rate that collapse came about quite abruptly. While Cressingham's men, in similar circumstances, had seventeen years before been trapped and slaughtered in the bend of the Forth, Edward's could and did burst out over the Pelstream and Bannockburn, albeit at terrible cost. The King himself and his immediate escort, very sensibly fought their way across the Pelstream and fled northwards across the carselands first towards Stirling Castle, and then around the rear of the Scots army to make their escape. The rest of the English army fared far worse. All of the English chroniclers stress how they were forced back into the 'great ditch' of the Bannockburn 'where a great part of our men perished'. Barbour goes so far as to claim that 'Bannock Burn betwixt the braes was so charged with horses and men that men might pass dry over it upon drowned horses and men'.

Those who did manage to get across seem to have been able to break contact and in some cases even manage something approaching an orderly withdrawal, for the Scots

*A convincing representation of a Scots archer from the Carlisle charter. Note the bare legs, hooded cloak and simple 'pot' helmet or 'steil bonnet'.*

became pre-occupied both with rounding up a substantial body of infantry who managed to get over the Pelstream to take refuge in Stirling – though not, it should be noted, in the castle, and, quite inevitably in plundering the English baggage train. A pursuit of sorts was organised under Douglas but seems not to have got beyond Winchburgh, although scattered bodies of fugitives were later killed or captured all over southern Scotland. Notwithstanding the apocalyptic scenes in the Bannockburn, contemporary English chronicles list only 154 knights killed or captured in the battle or afterwards, though this does not of course include ordinary cavalrymen not classed as gentlemen. In any case, once across the Bannockburn most of the mounted men will have been able to get away, but the fate of the anonymous infantry must have been far grimmer.

As to the Scots' losses, the only casualty of note was Sir John Graham of Airth and he was killed when the Earl of Atholl raided the baggage train at Cambuskenneth. On the battlefield itself there were certainly casualties caused by

**BANNOCKBURN**

**One Kilometre**

The defeat of the English: The caving-in of the English right flank is conjectural but suggested by the advent of the fresh Scots reserve division. The 'Small Folk' have been summoned forward to join in the battle, but while their arrival is encouraging to the Scots, the flat ground means the English may not be able to see them.

the English archers, whose shooting into the flank of Stewart's division was described as 'richt noisum', but otherwise there are not likely to have been many for the Scots' pikemen were fighting under optimum conditions. The inescapable fact is that Scotland's greatest victory over England was also probably the one won at least cost.

# Pinkie

Bannockburn, as Bruce had intended, set the seal on the recovery of Scotland's independence, although it was by no means the end of the war. After his death the so-called 'disinherited', led by Edward Balliol returned and, with the assistance of Edward III, took control of the country for a time. Ultimately their position was unsustainable and under the Stewart kings Scotland's independence was unchallenged again until the sixteenth century.

The trouble began with the disastrous Scots defeat at Flodden in 1513, and although the English had themselves been sufficiently battered there to set aside any notion of an invasion, Scotland took some considerable time to recover. For a long time afterwards the country was vulnerable to English raids. However, in 1542, some 500 English prisoners were taken at a battle at Haddon Rig, and when King James V refused to turn them loose, the Duke of Norfolk was ordered north to mount a substantial punitive raid. In the event his supply arrangements failed so completely that he was back in Berwick within a week. When James V responded in turn by sending a large army to invade Cumberland, an even more ignominious disaster resulted. Already riven by internal dissension the Scots army simply dissolved when it was ambushed by a far smaller force of English borderers on Solway Moss. Only about twenty were killed but 1,200 were captured and although he had not accompanied the army, the shock and humiliation effectively killed the King.

However, on 12 March 1543, less than three months after the King's untimely death, the Scots parliament, or Estates, accepted the offer of a marriage between their infant Queen, Mary, and Edward, the marginally less infant son and heir of King Henry VIII of England. It seemed an attractive way to settle accounts, but Henry overplayed his hand by reviving the old claim of suzerainty over Scotland and on 3 December the Scots not only broke off the engagement, but formally accepted a French alliance. Thereafter matters became somewhat complicated. Henry died in January 1547, but in his place the Lord Protector, the Earl of Hertford, tried to pressurise the Scots into accepting the marriage through a destructive series of border raids, which became known as 'The Rough Wooing'. Yet it was not a straightforward fight against English aggression for Protestantism had in the meantime spread to Scotland, sowing violent divisions between the Reformers and those who clung to the Catholic church. Only the year before a French envoy had noted that:

The Kingdom of Scotland was, and still is at the present time, under arms; for all the friends of one faction mistrust all those of the other faction; insomuch that not only the nobles are in arms, but churchmen, friars, and peasants travel through the country only in large companies, and all armed with jacks, swords, bucklers, and a half-pike in hand (which they call in this country a lance).

Increasingly, many on both sides of the divide were willing to make common cause with their co-religionists irrespective of nationality. That meant the Reformers or Protestants largely looked to England for support, while the Catholics looked to France. Nevertheless, when Hertford, having promoted himself to Duke of Somerset, embarked upon a full-blown invasion in September 1547, a temporary unity prevailed, but it was to be a sadly fragile one. Nowhere was this more apparent than in the way in which the Scots army was raised, for instead of requiring each sheriffdom to levy out its fencibles, the Earl of Arran, who was acting as Governor or Regent, sent round the fiery cross – asking in effect for volunteers.

Perhaps for that reason also it may have taken longer than expected to muster the army. On 22 August Somerset left London and by 1 September was at Berwick. Before crossing the border he tried to make the Scots an offer they could not refuse; proposing that after the marriage the Scots and English legal systems should remain independent, that free-trade and intermarriage should be allowed, but, in contrast, that the names of England and Scotland should be abolished and they should instead be united under an Emperor of Great Britain. Rather to his disappointment the Scots declined to send commissioners to discuss these imaginative proposals and so he headed north, not by the traditional route up Lauderdale but along the coast road, in order to be able to obtain supplies from an accompanying fleet.

This route had generally been avoided in the past since it passed through the dangerous defile or pass of Cockburnspath but, unlike the Edwards, he would not be able to rest and resupply at Leith, so there was no alternative. Rather to his relief however at the cost of only a little 'puffing and payne' Somerset passed safely through the defile and successively took and destroyed the small castles of Dunglas, Thornton and Innerwick, though avoiding the rather stronger ones at Dunbar and Tantallon. Not until 8 September did he find a formidable looking Scots army defending an equally formidable position, known as Edmonstone Edge, behind the river Esk at Musselburgh, just to the east of Edinburgh. Tradition used to place Somerset's camp on the high ground of Falside Hill, some three kilometres inland from the coast, but all of the contemporary chroniclers agree that after burning Tranent he encamped at Prestonpans, and one goes so far as to say that the English were 'at Salt Prestoun, als stronglie as they culd and neir unto the firth'. This latter point is confirmed by a useful series of contemporary drawings of the battle by a Scots Protestant named John Ramsay, which does indeed depict the English camp coming down almost to the beach on what is now Musselburgh race course.

However what the drawings also show is that instead of fighting with their

*The bridge and adjacent ford over the River Esk at Musselburgh crossed by Arran's and Huntly's divisions.*

camp to the rear, the English fought with it on their right flank, so the association with Falside Hill is correct after all, up to a point. What appears to have happened is that recognising the Scots army was well posted and stronger than his own, Somerset began by shuffling to the left in order to occupy the high ground of Falside Hill, but he was not destined to stay there long.

Although the Scots infantry remained behind the Esk, their cavalry, reported to be 1,500 strong could not 'abstene from daylie skarmusheing' and next morning were doing their very best to annoy the English, when Lord Grey of Wilton obtained permission to engage them. Grey chose his moment well and just as the Scots were turning for home, charged downhill at the head of his demi-lances, with some men at arms in support. The Scots, under Lord Home, faced about but were very quickly scattered. Home himself was knocked from his horse and trampled, before being rescued and bundled off to Edinburgh, but his son was captured along with six other gentlemen and two priests. Other losses are said to have been heavy and few of the rank and file are supposed to have escaped alive, which seems very unlikely given their well attested and rather sensible tendency to cut and run in times of adversity. Nevertheless, this action effectively destroyed the Scots cavalry and allowed Somerset to carry out a very close reconnaissance of Arran's position.

This soon convinced Somerset that a drastic change of plan was called for. The Scots obviously had no intention of attacking him, and it appeared impractical to outflank them by getting his army across the Esk below Falside Hill. Nevertheless he had to do something for having by-passed Dunbar and with the little harbour at Musselburgh still firmly in Scots hands, his accompanying fleet was unable to land any provisions.

Fa'side Castle

*Falside Hill (or Fawside Hill) - Somerset's original defensive position at Pinkie.*

*St Michael's Kirk at Inveresk as seen from the bridge.*

In the end he decided to make the most of his superiority in artillery by mounting his guns on Pinkie Cleuch, just forward of Inveresk Kirk. This is a fairly flat topped area of comparatively high ground (the plateau is at the twenty-five-metre contour) which forms a distinct salient with the river being diverted around three sides, and was also about five metres higher than the Scots' position on the opposite bank. It would therefore have made an admirable site for his artillery park and had the added advantage that he would be able to subject the Scots left wing to a heavy crossfire from both the Pinkie position and from his fleet just offshore. Once it had been thoroughly worked over, he would attack. Brushing off a Scots offer of an exchange of prisoners and safe conduct for a retreat, he resolved to put his plan into execution next morning, Saturday, 10 September 1547.

In order to take up position for his intended assault it was first necessary for Somerset to evacuate Falside Hill and concentrate the army on his right, just by the rather exposed camp. It was of course impossible to conceal this move from the Scots, but the Earl of Arran completely misinterpreted what he saw and leapt to the immediate conclusion that the English were preparing to withdraw. He may well have been encouraged in this belief by the way in which they were strung out. Some light cavalry led by Lord Ogle were posted by the camp, with a considerable gap between them and the three divisions of infantry, who were followed in turn by two brigades of demi-lances and men at arms.

Arran's plan was straightforward enough and with better management might well have succeeded. The Earl of Angus was to ford the river above Inveresk Kirk, and attack Somerset at once in order to gain time for the rest of the army to cross Musselburgh Bridge and cut Somerset's presumed line of retreat. Obviously however this cunning plan meant that Angus was going to have to bear the initial brunt of the battle on his own, but when he queried his rather peremptory instructions, they were repeated and he was ordered to go under pain of treason - which was hardly an auspicious start to the proceedings.

As so often happens, Somerset was so pre-occupied with organising his own attack that it never occurred to him that the Scots might seize the initiative, far less attack him before he was ready. Surprised both by the fact and the speed of the Scots advance, Somerset had to form 'front to flank' in great haste, and considerable confusion too for his guns were tangled up amongst his infantry.

The best estimates rather optimistically put his force at about 16,000 strong, which, if true, would be rather larger than just about every other English army to cross the border. Its composition was certainly different and reflected the rapidly changing face of warfare as the mediaeval period came to an end.

Armour had become considerably heavier and more expensive since the days of the Edwards, and the horses correspondingly so. Moreover, since Bannockburn English knights had generally fought in 'the Scottish fashion' – on foot – with the result that as one Italian commentator noted in 1557 that 'With regard to heavy horses, good for men at arms, the island does not produce any'. Instead, with the exception of a small band of Gentlemen Pensioners (not militant geriatrics but gentlemen soldiers, paid by the King and serving as a royal bodyguard) most English 'heavy' cavalry were so-called demi-lances, clad in fairly light three-

*Although this illustration dates from 1632 it provides a pretty fair idea of the appearance of the English heavy cavalry at Pinkie. Only the pistols are out of place.*

quarter armour. These were of course still more than heavy enough for service in Scotland but nevertheless Somerset, who was clearly a man for doing things by the book, sought to remedy the supposed deficiency by hiring a band of mercenary men-at-arms from the continent. The fact that their leader's name was Malatesta suggests they may have mainly been Italians, in which case they will have been true heavy lancers. However, many of the mercenary cavalry serving with the Tudor armies had been Burgundian or German reiters, armed with pistols. There were certainly some 'harquebusiers mounted', equipped with firearms, under another mercenary captain named Pedro de Gamboa, although it is not clear whether they were cavalrymen or mounted infantry.

In addition to these more or less exotic imports, who probably accounted for no more than about 200 men, Somerset also had perhaps as many as seventy Gentlemen Pensioners and up to 500 'Bulleners' – regular cavalrymen from the garrison of Boulogne. They, like the remainder of his cavalry, were a half and half mixture of demi-lances and northern 'prickers' or light cavalry, with a few mounted archers and arquebusiers. All in all, on the assumption that one in four of his men were mounted, secondary sources allow him a total of 4,000 cavalry but this is almost certainly too high and a more realistic estimation would probably be about 700 regular and mercenary cavalry, and another 2,000 demi-lances and prickers from the county levies.

As to Somerset's infantry, the majority were still armed with the traditional bills and bows. The actual proportions present at Pinkie appear to be unknown, but musters of those taken to France three years earlier show a ratio of about four archers to seven billmen, or 1:2 if a small but growing number of pikemen are added to the bills. Bows and bills or bows and pikes were banded together for administrative purposes into companies with a nominal strength of 100 officers and men, but in battle must have been consolidated into larger units within each division or 'regiment' and seem to have formed up with the billmen or pikemen in the centre and the archers on the flanks. Arquebusiers, or 'hackbutters', as they were more familiarly known on both sides of the border, were on the other hand formed into discrete companies and Somerset had five or six of them.

The usual wild confusion abounds over the strength and composition of the Scots army, though there is broad agreement it outnumbered the English. The most conservative estimate puts it at 23,000 men which is considerably larger than any other Scots army to take the field, with the dubious exception of the host James IV led to Flodden. As with the English army therefore a reduction of at least one third to about 15-16,000 men would still allow a comfortable superiority. Even this may be on the high side since allowing for the high proportion of cavalry in the English ranks it would still suggest an advantage of 2:1 in infantry. All that can be said with any certainty is that unlike most previous Scots armies they were substantially formed in three divisions under the Earls of Angus, Arran and Huntly, rather than the customary four. The first, according to John Knox, was comprised of 'the gentlemen of Fife, of Angus, Mearns, and the Westland'. The latter comprising the south-western shires of Lanark, Renfrew, Ayr, Wigton and Kirkcudbright. Arran's division was seemingly made up of contingents from Perthshire, Stirling, the Lothians, Teviotdale and the Merse, while Huntly's was drawn from

Aberdeenshire, Banffshire, Moray and Inverness.

Ramsay's drawings of the battle rather conventionally depict the three divisions as solid blocks of pikemen, and they may indeed have appeared thus from a distance. However closer examination reveals the interesting detail that the colours or banners flying over the three divisions are arranged in four groups which clearly indicates that each division was still made up of four individual schiltrons; two up and two back. In Angus' division for example the 'gentlemen of Fife' will have formed one schiltron, those of Angus and the Mearns another, and the 'Westland' men the other two.

The reason for this departure from previous practice is unclear but it may reflect the adoption of continental tactical doctrines and equipment which began during the Flodden campaign. The most obvious manifestation of this modernisation was the adoption of the 'Almayne' or *Landsknecht* pike, such as those carried by the Earl of Huntly's men who were noted in 1552 to be 'substantiouslie accompturit with jack and plait, steilbonnet, sword, bucklair... and a speir of sax elne long (5 metres) or thairby'. The longer pike allowed the use of a much deeper formation – some *Landsknecht* units were said to be twenty deep and supposedly therefore able to achieve much more impetus in the assault and any subsequent 'pushing'. In practice it turned out to be a rather dangerous innovation, for whilst very effective when used by well drilled troops fighting on level ground, both pikes and formations were unwieldly, easily stalled and very vulnerable to artillery and firearms.

In addition to the 12-15,000 pikemen there was also a large contingent of Highland clansmen, chiefly armed with bows, nominally attached to Huntly's division on the left but to all intents and purposes acting as a fourth division under the Earl of Argyle. After the previous day's debacle the remaining Scots cavalry were a negligible element, but there was also some artillery, at least four guns attached to Angus' and Huntly's divisions respectively, and a small park in the centre. Ramsay's drawings reveal the interesting detail that at least some of the Scots guns were of the fashionable double-barrelled variety – presumably imported from France.

Pitscottie's account of the battle includes an invaluable account of the army's movements, and relates how Angus went 'over the watter of

## ARTILLERY

By 1547 artillery had more or less developed to the level which, with constant refinements, it would maintain until the adoption of reliable breech-loading mechanisms and rifled barrels in the second half of the nineteenth century. No longer confined to siege work or fixed emplacements, guns could now be deployed on the battlefield, although it would also be fair to say that, generally speaking, they were still too heavy to be moved once they had been deployed. Both the English and Scots took great interest in the development of artillery, and Henry VIII had first bought the latest available guns abroad and then imported the gunfounders as well to work at factories in the Tower and at Houndsditch. The Scots had a similar operation in Edinburgh Castle. Field artillery, as distinct from siege artillery, was still at a very experimental stage and multi-barrelled pieces were common. Henry's gunmaker, Peter Baude, for example was making triple barrelled breech-loaders at Houndsditch in the 1530s, and contemporary sketches of Pinkie clearly show that most of the Scots guns were double-barrelled.

*The river at about the point where Angus' division crossed. The houses in the distance mark Edmonstone Edge, the original Scots position.*

Inveresk avastetelt the kirk thairof and stude in arrayit battell in the sight of his enemies till his ost and the governor [Arran] came ower the bredg to Mussillburgh and stude under an avastet the kirk of Inveresk and abone the fisheraw'.

In short, while Angus went straight across the river and uphill towards Somerset's column, Arran and Huntly crossed the bridge and forestalled Somerset by seizing the high ground by Inveresk kirk. Thanks to the lie of the ground Somerset was at first ignorant of their approach until the ships lying offshore alerted him by firing on Huntly's division as it emerged from behind the eastern

*This is the area in which Angus' division formed up after crossing the river. The fact that they were in dead ground at the time is strikingly apparent.*

*The flat expanse of Howe Mire looking towards Inveresk and Musselburgh. The spire of St. Michael's Kirk can be seen left of centre.*

end of Musselburgh. There were few casualties, but the gunfire seems to have been unexpected and a large number of the Highlanders attached to the division promptly took to their heels, while the pikemen shied off to their right and closed up against Arran's division in the centre.

In the meantime the Scots' right wing, commanded by the Earl of Angus, had crossed the river first and although 'they almost losed thair braithes or ever they culd cum to the joyning with the enemie', they were still coming on fast and notwithstanding a wealth of unfortunate precedence, Somerset ordered his heavy cavalry to attack them. Predictably enough they spectacularly came to grief, as related in one English account:

> The Scots stood at defence, shoulders nigh together, the fore-rank stooping low before, their fellows behind holding their pikes in both hands, the one end of the pike against the right foot, the other against the enemy's breast, so nigh as place and space might suffer. So thick were they that a bare finger should as easily pierce through the bristles of a hedgehog as any man encounter the front of the pikes.

Grey, who was himself wounded in the mouth simply complained afterwards that charging the Scots pikes was like running against a wall. It was indeed 'ane notabill owrthraw', casualties were heavy and Edward Shelley, the captain of the 'Bulleners' was killed together with a number of other gentlemen. Nevertheless Grey's charge had at least succeeded in halting Angus' division and Somerset now flung in his second heavy cavalry brigade, commanded by Sir Thomas Darcy, in a desperate attempt to gain time for his guns to be deployed. The Scots were unimpressed and as the armoured horsemen trotted down again, the pikemen taunted them with 'come here, loons! Come here, heretics!' and a Scots gunner

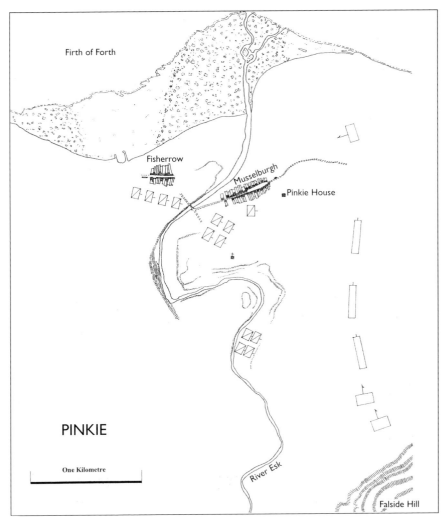

PINKIE

One Kilometre

Firth of Forth

Fisherrow

Musselburgh

Pinkie House

River Esk

Falside Hill

*Presumed dispositions at the moment when Somerset realised to his horror that the Scots were attacking while his army was strung out on the line of march. Angus' division is forming up in dead ground after fording the Esk. Arran's division is similarly halted awaiting the crossing of Huntly's division. Argyle's Highlanders are probing forward and about to come under fire from the English ships offshore.*

knocked Darcy off his horse. Despite the advantage of the slope the attack failed just as badly as the first and this time the English Royal Standard was nearly taken.

However both charges had achieved their purpose, for now Somerset had completed his battle-line. He had his guns in position and soon they were hammering the massed ranks of Scots pikemen at point blank range. At the same time the English archers and hackbutters also came up and began firing into the suddenly stalled schiltrons.

The Scots needed to get moving forward again, and had they done so might yet

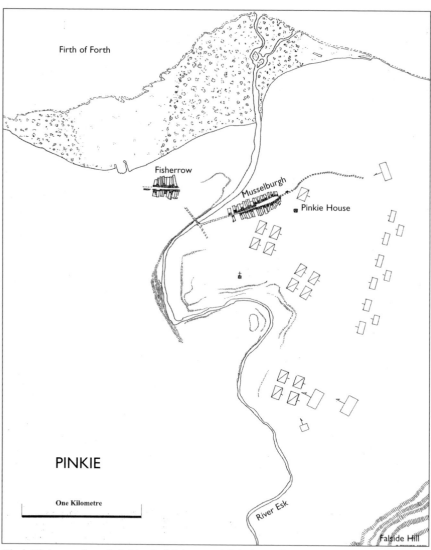

Firth of Forth

Fisherrow

Musselburgh

Pinkie House

**PINKIE**

One Kilometre

River Esk

Falside Hill

*The battle begun. Angus' division is fighting – and defeating – the English cavalry on Howe Mire. Arran has advanced beyond Inveresk Kirk, but is again waiting for Huntly's division to catch up. Somerset's infantry and artillery are now deployed, but likely to be overrun if the Scots advance can be properly co-ordinated.*

have carried the English position in one gallant rush. Ironically however they were prevented from doing so by the mounded bodies of men and horses piled across their front, and instead Angus decided to pull back and reorganise below the brow of the hill, while he waited for Arran and Huntly to get into the fight This turned out to be a bad mistake. In the first place it was by no means easy for such a large formation of pikemen to step backwards down the slope and although they at first managed it in tolerable order, halting them proved impossible and their formation began to fall apart.

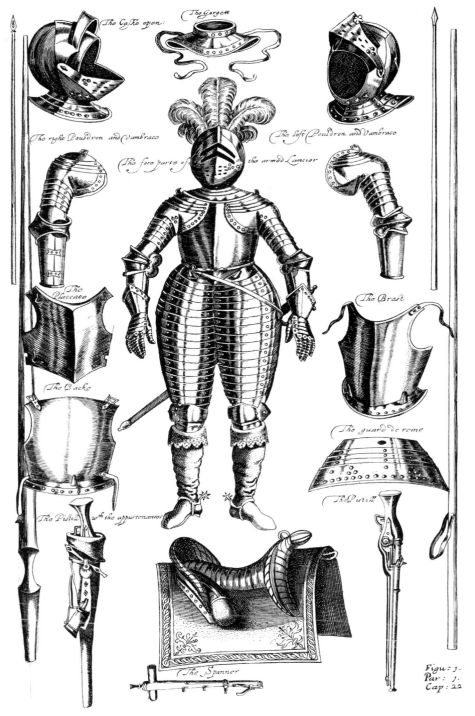

The Caske open. The Gorgett The right Pouldron and Vambraco The left Pouldron and Vambraco The fore parte of the armed Lancier The Placcate The Brest The Backe The guard de reine The Pistoll with the appurtenances The Pistoll The Spanner

Figu: 1.
Par: 1.
Cap: 22

*Arms and armour of a demi-lance as depicted by John Cruso in 1632, copying an illustration by Wallhausen of 30 years earlier, and, with the exception of the pistols, still providing a pretty fair impression of one of Somerset's heavy cavalrymen.*

Worse still, Angus was one of a number of Scots nobles said to be in English pay and when he saw him pulling back, Arran, who seems to have been a touch unstable and had earlier ordered him to advance under pain of treason, immediately leapt to the conclusion that he was betrayed. At this critical moment then he burst out with a despairing cry: 'Fy, fy! Treason!', then called for his horse and rode off to Edinburgh, leaving his army to its fate.

The battle of course was far from over at this point, but it was almost certainly lost beyond recovery. As the Scots hesitated Somerset ordered forward his billmen and pikemen, and Grey, having rallied his cavalry rather gamely led them on again. This forward movement, masked in part by a sudden heavy shower of rain, proved

*The monument to the battle of Pinkie, overlooking Howe Mire, the scene of the clash between Angus' division and the English cavalry.*

decisive. Even before the English infantry came up with them, Angus's division broke up completely and fled, followed by Arran's.

In the confusion Huntly's division, which still seems to have been lagging behind the others at first thought Arran's retreating men were the English, but they soon realised their mistake and fell back likewise. Huntly himself, too exhausted to run after marching some six kilometres in full plate armour, organised an ad hoc rearguard and stood for a time by the bridge until his little party was surrounded and forced to surrender, but his was the only resistance after the rout began.

As the schiltrons collapsed the men first threw away their unwieldy pikes, so that to one Englishman the ground at the foot of the bank looked like a wood-yard from the immense number of long pike-staves strewn on it. There were bodies enough as well once the English cavalry got in amongst the fugitives. Predictably enough a considerable number were killed or captured trying to cross the Esk, which proved to be a good deal more difficult the second time around. Thomas Maule of Panmure, who had fought in Angus' division certainly remembered the water was higher, which he attributed to its being dammed, but was more likely due to the tide having come it. Consequently those who crossed had their clothing so thoroughly soaked as to make them 'heavie and onabil to flea'.

Panmure was one of the luckier ones, having reached the other side he immediately stripped off his jack and ran for it, sword in hand. The English cavalry were not in the mood to grant quarter and crying out 'Remember Peniel Heugh!' – their name for a grievous defeat on Ancrum Moor the year before – they set about the fugitives unmercifully. No quarter was certainly given to any of the numerous Catholic priests who had marched on to the battlefield behind a white sarsnet banner bearing a picture of a maiden representing the Church kneeling before

*Highland archer of Huntly's division.*

Christ, with the motto *Ne Obliviscaris Domine Sponsae Afflictae* (Forget not Thy afflicted Bride, O Lord), and were clearly the lineal forebears of those religious zealots who would so afflict Scotland's soldiers a century later.

The numbers of dead were far more considerable, though even the most modest estimate of some 8,000 is probably too high. Nevertheless they included three lords and a large number of gentlemen, including seven sons of Sir Thomas Urquhart of Cromartie. The evidence of the Exchequer Rolls and other legal documents shows at least 80 landed gentlemen killed, more than half of them from Angus' division. It was noted in fact that for once the gentlemen were cut down as readily as the common soldiers, not through design but simply because they too were wearing jacks, or had covered any plate armour with white leather and were thus indistinguishable. All in all only five gentlemen were amongst the 1,000 or so prisoners taken, including the Master of Home who had actually been captured the day before.

English losses were of course much lower and probably amounted to something between 250 and 500, mainly amongst the cavalry who flung themselves against Angus' division.

Notwithstanding the magnitude of the Scots' defeat, which was widely compared to Flodden thirty years before, the battle was politically something of an anti-climax. Somerset burned Leith and then went home, leaving the projected union of the two crowns in abeyance until James VI quietly came into possession of the English throne in 1603. It was also the last battle to be fought between the Scots and the English until the Great Civil War erupted in 1639 and, by then, the face of warfare had changed markedly.

*English captain of foot as depicted in a contemporary watercolour sketch.*

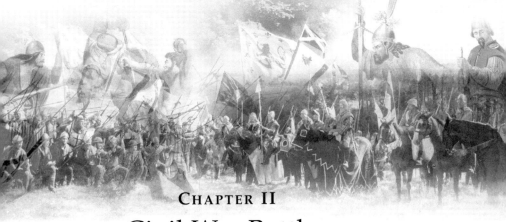

## CHAPTER II
# Civil War Battles

### *Warriors: Civil War Soldiers*

The century which separated the Battle of Pinkie from Scotland's involvement in the Great Civil War of the mid-seventeenth century witnessed a remarkable change in infantry tactics. If the medieval period was dominated by pikemen, the Civil Wars were dominated by the gun.

There were, as we have seen, some musketeers at Pinkie, but not in sufficient numbers to have a significant effect on the way in which the battle was fought, far less its outcome. However in the years which followed improvements in technology and manufacturing capabilities saw the proportions of musketeers to other soldiers rise dramatically and with them came a revolution in the way battles were fought.

By 1645, when the Marquis of Montrose met Lieutenant General William Baillie at Kilsyth, the musket itself was still a fairly unsophisticated device comprising an iron tube mounted on a wooden stock. It was loaded simply by pouring a measure of gunpowder and a spherical lead ball down the muzzle end and tamping both down with the weapon's 'scouring stick' which doubled as a ramrod. The lock or firing mechanism, comprised a sear which when acted upon by a lever lowered a clamp holding a slow-burning fuse known as 'match' down on to a priming charge in a small pan attached to the breech end of the barrel. When the match ignited this priming charge the resultant flame flashed through a small hole in the side of the barrel to ignite the main charge within.

Notwithstanding its apparent crudity the matchlock musket was on the whole a robust and reliable weapon, and one moreover which could be mastered within a very short period of time. It would be no exaggeration to say that whilst the famed English longbowman had virtually to be trained up from birth, a passably competent musketeer could be turned out in an afternoon. This indeed was the key to the demise of the longbow, for good archers were professional soldiers drawn from the sons of yeoman farmers and by this period they had forsaken the bow for the horse. The lineal descendants of the bowmen who made such a sad havoc of the Scots pikemen at Falkirk, Halidon Hill and Flodden were not the peasant musketeers of Cromwell's army, but his Ironsides.

The musket certainly had its shortcomings, but these were well recognised at the time and mitigated by the drills devised for its use.

The first drawback of the weapon was its very size. Most gun barrels were about 1.219 metres (4 feet) long which meant that when the butt was rested upon the ground the muzzle stood just above the soldier's shoulder. Naturally enough this made the musket very awkward to load in an upright position, but this particular problem was overcome by swinging the gun around by the left side at an angle of between forty and forty-five degrees. Loading then becomes comparatively easy, but the need to swing the musket back and forth meant that far from standing shoulder to shoulder like pikemen, musketeers needed plenty of space around them.

The second limitation was the time which was required to reload it. On the word of command the soldier had first to swing his gun down by his side, open a powder flask and pour a measure of gunpowder down the barrel. He would then fish in his pocket for a bullet to send after it, draw his scouring stick from its slot in the underside of the stock, insert it too in the barrel and tamp down the ammunition, then removing and returning it. Then, bringing the musket up in front of him, he would dribble some fine grade powder from another flask into the flash pan, shut it and attach the slow-match to the clamp. Complicated though this procedure sounds a reasonably proficient musketeer could easily accomplish it with thirty seconds.

Nevertheless, recognising the vulnerability of the musketeer while he reloaded his piece, officers initially deployed their men in six ranks. The first rank would fire then fall back to the rear to reload, followed in due succession by the other five. The theory was that by the time the last rank had fired the men in the first would be standing ready to start the cycle afresh. This military ballet no doubt looked very impressive on a parade ground, but looked a great deal less pretty on a battlefield and bitter experience saw the line thin out sometimes to three or four deep or for each man to stay where he was. They might still fire by ranks, but it became increasingly common to fire off all the available muskets in a salvee, or massed volley, and then follow it up with a charge.

Either way the requirement to give the musketeer plenty of room in which to reload, whether or not he first passed through the ranks to do so in the rear, led to seventeenth-century battlefields becoming much more linear than medieval ones.

Nevertheless, neither the pikeman nor the schiltron actually disappeared from Scottish battlefields during this period, but their importance was very much diminished. Infantry were now organised in regiments which generally varied in strength between 200 and 700 men and were deployed with a schiltron of pikemen in the centre and a wing of musketeers on either side. The actual proportion of pikemen to musketeers in each regiment depended on the availability of firearms, but even at the outset of the Civil Wars musketeers never accounted for less than half of a regiment's strength and by the battle of Dunbar in 1650 they normally amounted to two thirds. Consequently the role of the pikemen changed. Instead of quite literally spearheading assaults they were now held back until the opposition had first been thoroughly softened up by the musketeers. This in turn meant that in the early stages of the battle the fighting could be quite static, but on the other hand the succeeding assault phase was now much faster and more violent.

As in the medieval period the importance of cavalry depended upon the circumstances and the ground being favourable for their use. Scots armies continued to suffer from a shortage of the large and heavy horses favoured by their English counterparts and consequently tended to operate as light horse lancers. Cavalry were fairly effective against infantry, especially if their superior mobility was employed in getting in on the flank or rear of the infantry formation. The only real defence which the infantry could offer was still to close up tight and depend on their pikes, but while this was generally effective enough in itself the musketeers sheltering under those pikes were unable to reload and both therefore were vulnerable to a simultaneous assault by infantry.

Artillery remained tactically insignificant. The technology had improved considerably over the years and indeed Scots artillerists devised a species of very useful pack-mounted guns called 'frames', but the simple fact of the matter was that an absence of good roads in Scotland meant that only the lightest of cannon could be brought to the battlefield.

**EXPERIENCES OF WAR**

*Continued...*

*Glenlivet. All this was in addition to the constant small change of feuds which involved skirmishes ranging in size from petty brawls to full scale battles. There was also a long-standing Scots mercenary tradition, and in the first half of the seventeenth century thousands of Scots served abroad, chiefly in the Dutch and Swedish armies. On the outbreak of war at home the Scots' government recognising the value of this pool of experience, invited the mercenaries to return and ensured they were well paid. Until such time as locally recruited officers were sufficiently well trained the Scots army also introduced a system whereby the commander of a regiment would be a nobleman, but his second in command would be a professional. Similarly while a local laird would be appointed a captain to lead out his men in time honoured fashion, he would again be given an experienced soldier to act as his lieutenant.*

# Kilsyth

In 1603 the death of the childless Queen Elizabeth left the King of Scots as the heir to the English throne. Eager to escape the endless round of intrigue, attempted coups and assassinations which passed for court life in Scotland, King James VI hurried southwards with almost indecent haste to assume his inheritance. Scotland meanwhile remained an entirely separate country and his son, Charles I, preferring to base himself in his richer southern kingdom, took little interest in Scots affairs until his belated coronation in 1633.

His father, once dubbed the 'Wisest fool in Christendom', knew well enough when to leave matters alone, but his thoroughly anglicised son misjudged his subjects disastrously. Two generations earlier Scotland had firmly embraced the Protestant Reformation, but the King now decided to reverse that conversion by remodelling the Scots Kirk on Episcopalian or High Anglican lines. Bishops would be appointed by the King and they in turn, not the local presbyteries, would appoint the ordinary clergy. To the Scots this proposal was unpopular enough in itself, but worse was to come.

In order to finance the proposed reforms, and in particular the hierarchy of bishops that was to be reinstated in place of the democratic Presbyterian system, Charles also announced his intention of re-possessing the former landholdings of the Catholic church. At the Reformation these vast lands had fallen to the Crown and then largely been sold on to the great benefit of the Exchequer. Now Charles intended that they should revert to the Crown and although compensation was promised, he was all but bankrupt and this was widely regarded as unlikely to materialise. Moreover, in a culture in which the number of a man's tenants was accounted of more worth than more material indicators of wealth, the potential loss of those tenants was a serious matter indeed. The result was that the proposed religious reforms not only alienated the population at large, but by directly threatening the wealth and above all the power of the nobility, they also provided the people with leaders.

In 1638 a National Covenant pledged a substantial part of the population, great and small, to oppose the King's reforms and in 1639 and 1640 the brief and inglorious 'Bishops' Wars' saw Scotland's independence very firmly re-asserted. From then onwards although lip-service was still paid to the King as the titular head of state, Scotland was a republic in all but name, and it was as a sovereign power that her government agreed to support the Westminster Parliament in the English Civil War which followed. Under the terms of the Solemn League and Covenant of 1643 Scotland was committed to enter that war with an army of over 20,000 men. Intervention on such a scale would be fatal to the English Royalist cause and so at the King's headquarters a plan was set in train to knock Scotland back out of the war before it was too late.

The principal actor was to be James Graham, Marquis of Montrose, who had once been a very prominent Covenanter before ending up on the wrong side of the political fence. There were three main elements to this plan. Montrose himself was to lead a motley collection of Scots mercenaries and English levies northwards across the border to raise a rebellion in Dumfries and the old Catholic south-west. In the north-east of Scotland, the long time Royalist, George Gordon, Marquis of Huntly, was to lead a similar rebellion, while in the west, Randal MacDonnell, Earl of Antrim, was pledged to bring an army across from Ireland.

Only Huntly played his part at the appointed time. He raised his followers as promised and took over Aberdeen. The Irish were late and Montrose, also arriving rather too late on the scene, briefly occupied Dumfries before being ignominiously chased back across the border considerably quicker than he had come. Isolated, Huntly was forced to fly for his life and ever afterwards considered himself betrayed by Montrose. The Marquis, for his part, rode south to beg more men from the King's nephew, Prince Rupert, but on 2 July 1644 the English Royalists' northern army was smashed by an Anglo-Scots army on Marston Moor outside York. Rupert had no regiments to spare and so Montrose slipped home to Scotland without a single man at his back.

In the meantime Antrim's Irish mercenaries had sailed after all and landed in Ardnamurchan on 8 July. The brigade is frequently assumed to have been almost entirely comprised of exiled MacDonald clansmen, but only three of the companies can be identified as such. The remainder were raised in various parts of Ireland and commanded by experienced officers – some of whom had previously served in the Spanish army

### MONTROSE

*Assessments of the Marquis of Montrose's abilities tend to be excessively coloured by the heroic account of his campaigns written by his personal chaplain, George Wishart, and a more balanced appreciation raises some serious questions. There is no doubt whatsoever that he was the very epitome of the dashing cavalier - or that he showed dogged determination in the face of adversity. Unfortunately, all too often, that determination bordered on a single-minded fanaticism which alienated many potential supporters, and, worse still, blinded him to the necessities of proper intelligence-gathering reconnaissance and most other practical aspects of the professional soldier's trade. His victories tended to be balanced by some spectacular debacles such as being pounced upon by Baillie while plundering Dundee and being caught completely unawares at Auldearn. Luck and the exertions of his rather more capable subordinate, Alasdair MacCholla, saved him on both occasions and perhaps also in the rather untidily fought battle at Kilsyth. Ultimately his carelessness led directly to his subsequent defeat at Philiphaugh and the yet more disastrous debacle at Carbisdale.*

*James Graham, Marquis of Montrose – the King's general.*

in Flanders. They were for the most part armed with muskets and pikes. Oddly enough their commander was not an Irishman but a Hebridean Scot, Alasdair MacCholla. The eldest son of Coll MacDonald of Colonsay, whose nickname Coll Coitach (or Colkitto) he often shares, he was a professional soldier who had fought on both sides (twice) in the bloody Irish rebellion before being given command of Antrim's mercenaries and sent to Scotland. Often portrayed as a stout but not overly-intelligent foil to Montrose's brilliance, he was actually a very capable soldier whose only real 'failing' lay in his ambition to set himself up as an independent warlord and to embark upon a doomed attempt to re-establish Clan Donald's hegemony in the Isles.

In the meantime, finding himself in the classic situation of a mercenary officer stranded without an employer in a hostile countryside, he began searching for the King's general. The mercenaries found him at Blair Atholl on 29 August 1644 and so the great adventure began. Just three days later they defeated the government's hastily assembled forces on Tibbermore, just outside Perth. Two weeks afterwards they destroyed another army outside Aberdeen, but then sacked the burgh so thoroughly as to destroy any hope of enlisting its citizens in the King's cause. In October the rebels came close to being trapped by the Marquess of Argyle's forces at Fyvie Castle in Aberdeenshire, but bounced back with a raid into Argyllshire and spent Christmas at his castle of Inverary. In the new year, after a dramatic march over the mountains in midwinter, they destroyed yet another army at Inverlochy, close by what is now Fort William, on Candlemas day, but then very nearly overreached themselves in April with a raid on Dundee which went disastrously wrong.

The Scots government had responded to the growing Royalist threat by withdrawing a number of veteran regiments from England. Just as Montrose and his men broke into the burgh and began dispersing in search of plunder, breathless word came that some of those veterans led by Lieutenant General William Baillie were closing in fast. Reputedly the Royalists fled by the burgh's East Port while Baillie's cavalry came galloping in through the West Port. Eventually, under cover of darkness, they succeeded in breaking contact and escaping into the hills. From then on however the battles which Montrose faced were to be much stiffer.

After this debacle at Dundee, Baillie's second in command, an engaging rogue named Sir John Hurry, was sent northwards to rally support for the government in the north-east. In the event the Royalists found him first, but he skilfully withdrew to Inverness conducting a classic rearguard action, until snapping back with a sudden counter-attack on the morning of 9 May 1645. He quite literally caught the

Royalists napping at Auldearn, near Nairn. He had been reinforced by the Inverness garrison and the northern levies assembled by the Earls of Seaforth and Sutherland, and what turned out to be the hardest fought battle of the war raged all day before his army was defeated in a dramatic series of counter-attacks. Hurry withdrew with what remained under cover of darkness and the Royalists were no doubt glad to see him go for it had been a pyrrhic victory. Instead of pursuing the remnants of Hurry's army and seizing Inverness, they too withdrew, so hampered by a long train of wounded that it took all day to pass them over the river Spey.

While MacCholla was away recruiting in the West Highlands, Baillie again caught up with the rebels at Alford in Aberdeenshire. Once again the fighting was hard but in the end the Royalist cavalry prevailed and after defeating Baillie's troopers, settled the business by getting into the rear of his infantry.

This time the result was decisive. Thus far Montrose had won a succession of victories only to be threatened by fresh forces before he could consolidate his gains, but now the government appeared to be running out of soldiers. He on the other hand was master of a substantial part of Scotland and was able to gather his forces for a final offensive aimed at breaking through to the rich Lowlands and at last relieving the pressure on the King, who had himself just suffered at catastrophic defeat at Naseby in Northamptonshire.

Nevertheless it was a slow business. Huntly's eldest son, Lord Gordon, who had defected to the Royalists with a regular cavalry regiment at the beginning of the year and then called out his father's tenants in the King's service, was killed at Alford and leadership of the Gordons then passed to his younger brother, Lord Aboyne. An even more committed Royalist than his dead brother, Aboyne readily agreed to march south but first insisted on raising more men. In the meantime he extracted a promise from Montrose that he would not fight until reinforced – which rather suggests the Marquis's colleagues were by now rather wary of his unfortunate predilection for rushing into fights without adequate reconnaissance.

Unfortunately he then proceeded to do just that. At Fordoun in the Mearns, Alasdair MacCholla rejoined him with 1,400 men of the western clans and 200 Athollmen under Patrick Graham of Inchbrackie. Encouraged by this substantial accession of strength Montrose, instead of waiting for Aboyne and his Gordons, immediately essayed a raid on Perth and was lucky to get away when Baillie, who had scraped together another army, came after him and chased the Royalists back into the hills. Less lucky were the camp-followers caught by Baillie's cavalry and massacred in Methven Woods.

Of itself it was a small affair, but exasperated by his failure to catch Montrose's soldiers, and by what he regarded as constant political interference in military operations, Baillie then resigned as commander of the army. A very competent soldier, Baillie actually performed rather better than he is often given credit for when given a free hand, but he had a pathological inability to cope with his political masters – a trait which would eventually be just as apparent at Preston in 1648 as it was to be in 1645. Initially he had been very successful in out-manoeuvring Montrose and had come dangerously close to capturing him at Dundee, but on the battlefield he was more than a touch unfortunate. He appears to have been one of those generals who could bring his army on to an advantageous position on the battlefield but then had very little idea what to do with it once he'd got it there. Whilst his problems with political operators and appointees command a certain sympathy, perhaps his greatest failing was a tendency to respond to them by abdicating any and all responsibility for anything – a trait which was to become all too apparent in the coming days.

In the meantime the government for its part accepted his 'dimission' but then prevailed upon him to effectively serve out his notice until a replacement, Major General Robert Monro, could be fetched home from Ireland. In the meantime Aboyne at last came south to rendezvous with Montrose at Dunkeld, bringing with him 400 cavalry and 800 good infantry to take

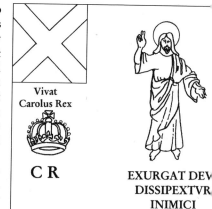

*Colour carried by one of the Irish mercenary companies – yellow with a red saltire in the canton – this may have been the yellow banner carried MacCholla's men at Auldearn.*

part in the culminating act of the campaign.

As Montrose pushed southwards once more, Baillie dug in at Bridge of Earn only for the rebels to by-pass his fortified camp and head for the Mills of Forth on 11 August. Delayed by an errant infantry brigade which incontinently marched home to Fife, and a memorable falling out with his political masters, Baillie was slow in getting after them, but he crossed Stirling Bridge on 14 August and promptly had yet another acrimonious row with his superiors. By now, however, it was clear that the rebels were heading towards Glasgow rather than Edinburgh and Baillie's scouts soon reported them to be encamped near Kilsyth on a high meadow overlooking the Glasgow road.

Next morning, learning that the rebels were still sitting there it was decided to go after them. Very sensibly, Baillie left the road and, as he explained in a remarkable dossier of evidence produced at the subsequent inquiry, 'marched with the regiments through the corns and over the braes, untill the unpassable ground did hold us up'. 'There I imbattled' – either along the line of the present unclassified road running from the A803 at Kelvinhead to Banton or more likely slightly further forward behind Girnal Hill – 'where I doubt if on any quarter twenty men on a front could either have gone from us or attack us'.

*Colour carried by one of the Irish mercenary companies – plain white with a blood red cross in the centre. The canton is yellow with a red saltire.*

The Royalists meanwhile were for some reason still lying on the high ground to the north of the Glasgow road. Consequently Baillie now discovered that his army was actually sitting on the rebels' exposed left flank, and if he could but accomplish it, poised to inflict a memorable defeat. The problem was of course the 'unpassible' ground:

> At the upcoming of the noblemen and others of the Committee, whom I dow not so weell remember, It was asked of my by the Lords, but by whom in particular I have forgott, If we could not draw up to the hill on our right hand? I shew them I did not conceive that ground to be good, and that the rebels (if they would) might possess themselves of it before us. Their Lordships then desired that some might be sent to visit the ground; which was done. In the meantime I went with my Lord Elcho and Burghlie to the right hand of the regiments. Not long after, I wes sent for by the other noblemen, and I desired the Lord Elcho and Burghlie to go with me, conjecturing they would press our removing; which at our coming they did, alleadging the advantage might be had of the enemies from that field, they being, as they supposed, allready on their march westward. I liked not the motion: I told them, if the rebels should seek to engadge us there I conceaved they should have great advantage of us; farder if we should beat them to the hill, it would be unto us no great advantage.

Although he thus stressed his misgivings about the move there was actually no real alternative but to continue the inadvertent turning movement by striking northwards and seizing the high ground at Auchinrivoch.

To accomplish it Baillie had about 300 troopers of the Earl of Balcarres' Regiment and another sixty newly levied ones belonging to Colonel Harie Barclay's. He also had a total of some 3,500 infantry. The best of them belonged to his five regiments of regulars: Argyle's, a regular regiment, raised in the lowlands, which had been garrisoning Berwick on Tweed and should not be confused with Argyle's Highland regiment which fought at Inverlochy; the Earl of Crawford-Lindsay's; Colonel Robert Home's red-coated veterans from Ireland; the Earl of Lauderdale's; and 'three that were joyned in one'. The latter, only some 300-strong comprised the remnants of the Earl of Cassillis', the Earl of Glencairn's and the Lord Chancellor's regiments, all hardened veterans who had survived Alford or Auldearn. The three remaining regiments on the other hand other were newly levied units from Fife under the lairds of Fordell, Ferny and Cambo. All three regiments had earlier tried to disband themselves and return home in the face of the Royalist offensive and although they had been rounded up and fetched back again, no-one, understandably, had very much confidence in them.

At the outset of the battle a picked battalion of musketeers commanded by Major John Haldane of the Lord Chancellor's Regiment stood on the right together with Balcarres' cavalry. They would lead the advance on the hill. Next came Lauderdale's Foot, then Home's and Argyle's. For lack of space Crawford-Lindsay's and the 'three joyned in one' initially flanked the three Fife regiments in the second line, but they did not stay there long.

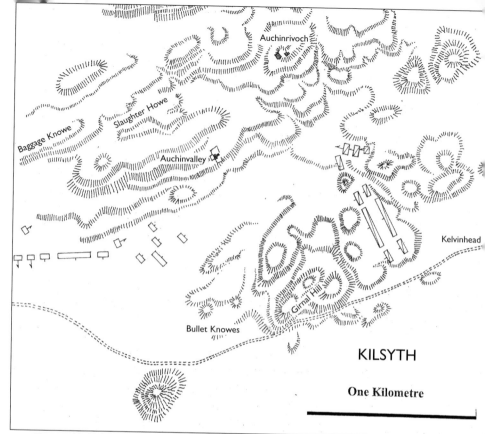

*Presumed initial dispositions with Baillie's army deployed behind Girnal Hill and Montrose's regulars about two kilometres further west, although his Highlanders are moving up the glen between Auchinvalley and Bullet Knowes.*

Initially the move went well enough. Many secondary sources deride it as having been foolishly carried out in full view of the Royalists, but as Baillie's own very detailed account makes clear, his army was at this point in time lying on a reverse slope and therefore almost completely hidden from the rebels. Nevertheless by now Montrose's men, no doubt alerted by the sight of horsemen and scouts hovering on their flank, were becoming uncomfortably aware that something was going on.

It is difficult to be very certain as to how the rebels were actually drawn up since the appearance of Baillie's men on their flank threw them into considerable confusion – rather more confusion in fact than they afterwards admitted. There were about 500 Irish mercenaries forming two battalions under Colonel Thomas Laghtnan and Colonel Manus O'Cahan; a brigade of 800 Gordons under Colonel James Farquharson of Inverey, comprising his own 'standing' (ie. regular) regiment, the veteran Strathbogie Regiment and Colonel William Gordon of Monymore's Regiment; and 200 Athollmen under Patrick Graham of Inchbrackie.

All of these men, 1,500 in all. were well armed and reasonably well trained and disciplined, but in addition Alasdair MacCholla had brought in 1,400 men of the western clans. In total therefore the Royalists had rather fewer infantry, but this was to be more than offset by their surprising superiority in cavalry: 360 troopers belonging to Lord Aboyne's and Colonel Nathaniel Gordon's regiments, eighty more belonging to the Earl of Airlie's, and about 200 dragoons or mounted infantry. Moreover the greater number of them were not the 'bonnet lairds on cart horses' of popular legend, but former regulars who had defected at the beginning of the year and since gained themselves a formidable reputation at Auldearn and Alford.

Having set his men off, Baillie decided to check on the rebels and 'galloped over the brae to see the posture of the enemie, who were embattled in the meadow and sundries of them disbanded were falling up the glen through the bushes.' This was a worrying development, but at least since Baillie could see their main body still standing in the meadow, he could be reassured that they were neither making off, nor racing his men to the Auchinrivoch position.

Baillie had intended that his march should be screened by the composite battalion of musketeers commanded by Major Haldane, but when they broke cover a short distance to the north of their starting point, they were spotted immediately by those straggling rebels 'falling up the glen'. At that point, to Baillie's horror, Haldane decided that he could best carry out the spirit if not the letter of his instructions by establishing himself in the farm at Auchinvalley. The challenge was immediately accepted by a rebel officer named Ewen Maclean of Treshnish. A spirited skirmish began around the farm enclosures and despite Baillie's repeated orders to disengage it soon began to escalate in intensity as MacDonnell of Glengarry led up his men to reinforce Treshnish.

*Slaughter Howe and Baggage Knowe as seen from the western end of Girnal Hill and the Bullet Knowes. The glen lying between is now flooded by a reservoir. Note the very high ground beyond.*

Initial Royalist position.

*Another view of the battlefield from a point just to the west of Girnal Hill. Auchinvalley, the scene of the fiercest fighting can be seen at middle distance in the centre. It is likely that some of Montrose's regular troops passed over this ground to attack Baillie's reserve brigade near Girnal Hill.*

Recognising that for good or ill the battle was now well and truly begun, Baillie rode to the front with his cavalry commander, the Earl of Balcarres. In his later evidence he provided both a unique insight into the sequence and nature of the orders given, and also more than a flavour of the confusion and excitement as his army, far from being helplessly swept away as it was strung out on the line of march, actually moved resolutely into the attack:

> Seeing the rebells fall up strong I desired them [the lords] to reteire, and the officers to goe to their charge. My Lord Balcarras and I galloped back to the

*Girnal Hill as seen from the Bullet Knowes. Although Baillie is tolerably vague on this point in his narrative it seems likely that John Leslie's Fife brigade was posted on the hill and attacked there by Royalist infantry advancing across the boggy area in the foreground.*

regiments. He asked me what he should do? I desired him to draw up his regiment on the right hand of the Earl of Lauderdale's. I gave order to Lauderdale's both by myselfe and my adjutant, to face to the right hand, and to march to the foot of the hill, then to face as they were; to Hume to follow their steps, halt when they halted, and keep distance and front with them. The Marquess [of Argyle] his Major, as I went toward him asked what he should doe? I told him, he should draw up on Hume's left hand, as he had done before. I had not ridden farr from him, when looking back, I find Hume had left the way I put him in, and wes gone at a trott, right west, in among the dykes and toward the enemy.

First Baillie's attempt to seize the Auchinrivoch position had been sidetracked by the untimely initiative of one subordinate, now another was compounding the error by rushing to his support. Most secondary sources assume that MacCholla's highlanders quickly overran Haldane's musketeers and then swept on to attack the rest of Baillie's army as it was strung out on the line of march. Instead, as Baillie's detailed account all-too vividly makes clear command and control on both sides was rapidly breaking down as the two armies rushed piecemeal into an encounter battle which neither had intended. Baillie continues:

I followed [Home] alse fast as I could ride and meeting the Adjutant on the way, desired him he should bring up the Earl of Crafurd's regiment to Lauderdale's left hand, and cause the Generall-Major [John] Leslie draw up the regiments of Fyfe in reserve as of before; but before I could come to Hume, he and the other two regiments, to wit, the Marquess of Argyles and the three that were joyned in one, had taken in an enclosure, from whilk [the enemy being so neer] it wes impossible to bring them off.

Instead of straggling along in a column, his army was now drawn up in three distinct bodies facing the enemy. Under his personal command up amongst the stone or turf-walled enclosures by Auchinvalley were some 1,600 regulars. Behind Baillie and to his right were a further 800 infantry under Major General Holbourne, and Balcarres' 300 cavalry, whilst somewhere to his left rear were the three rather shaky Fifeshire regiments under Major General Leslie.

In the meantime, immediately facing him were just 1,400 or so Highlanders under MacCholla – pinned down for the moment on the far side of the Auchinvalley enclosures:

The rebels foot, by this time, were approached the next dyke, on whom our musqueteers made more fire than I could have wished; and therefore I did what I could, with the assistance of such of the officers as were known unto me, to make them spare their shott till the enemy should be at a nearer distance, and to keep up the musqueteers with their pickes and collors, but to no great purpose.

Baillie then went on to recall how the Royalists 'in the end' overwhelmed his men, but for the moment the clansmen were well and truly pinned down behind the

dyke on the far side of the enclosure and all was going to depend on what happened further to the north on what had now become Baillie's right wing. Alexander Lindsay, Earl of Balcarres, was a competent and determined cavalry officer and now he did his best to hook around into the Royalist rear. At first all that stood in his path was a small troop of cavalry commanded by a 'Captain Adjutant' Gordon. Undaunted by the odds, the Royalists immediately charged and briefly checked Balcarres' advance. However the imbalance in numbers soon told against them, but just as they were on the point of being surrounded, Aboyne came to their aid with his personal lifeguard.

It was obviously an adventurous ride for sheering away from Harie Barclay's as yet unengaged lancers, the Royalists collided momentarily with the pikemen of Home's 'reid' regiment, and were shot up by its flanking musketeers before finally reaching Gordon's beleaguered troop. Unsurprisingly, by then they were in pretty poor shape and Balcarres drove them all back and up on to the high ground behind Montrose's original battle-line. There at last the Covenanters were halted when Nathaniel Gordon and the Earl of Airlie counter-attacked with the main body of the Royalist cavalry. Ominously the area is still marked on modern maps as 'Slaughter Howe'. Tired and badly outnumbered, Balcarres and his men were tumbled back down the hill again and completely out of the fight. Worse still, the victorious Royalist troopers then turned on the now-exposed right flank of Baillie's infantry and so at last provided the opportunity for MacCholla and his Highlanders to mount another frontal attack.

The end when it came was dramatic and once again, it was Baillie himself who provided the most vivid account of what followed:

*Highland clansman – one of a number of mercenaries sketched in Stettin in the early 1630s.*

In the end the rebells leapt over the dyke, and with downe heads fell on and broke these regiments... The present officers whom I remember were Home, his Lieutenant Colonel and Major of the Marquess's regiment, Lieutenant Colonel Campbell, and Major Menzies, Glencairne's sergeant Major, and Cassillis's Lieutenant Colonel with sundry others who behaved themselves well, and whom I saw none carefull to save themselves before the routing of the regiments. Thereafter I rode to the brae, where I found Generall Major

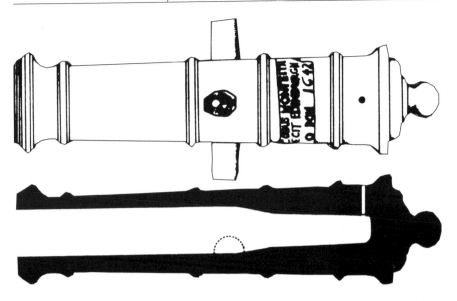

*Baillie had some of these light pack-mounted guns at Kilsyth, and also a larger piece captured from English Royalists at Marston Moor and named Prince Robert.*

Hollburne alone, who shew me a squadron of the rebells horsemen, who had gone by and charged the horsemen with Lieutenant-Colonell Murray (Barclay's Regiment) and, as I supposed, did afterward rowt the Earle of Crawfurd, and these with him.

With his front line overwhelmed by the rebel infantry, and Crawford-Lindsay's and Lauderdale's regiments dispersed by the rebel cavalry, Baillie and Holburne 'galloped through the inclosures to have found the reserve; bot before we could come at them, they were in flight'.

It would be easy to imply that Leslie's Fife brigade simply broke and ran without putting up any kind of resistance. Although there are no contemporary accounts of this particular episode, Baillie explicitly if indirectly refers to some kind of a fight when replying to accusations that his men were so ill-prepared that they had not time to light the slow-match for their muskets before the rebels attacked:

The fire given by the first five regiments will sufficiently answer what concerns them: and for the other three (the Fife levies), I humbly intreat your Honours to inform yourselves of Generall-Major Leslie, the adjutant, and the chief officers of these severall regiments: if they doe not satisfie yow therein, then I shall answer for myself.

With the rebel cavalry all engaged on the northern side of the battlefield and MacCholla's highlanders fully occupied in dealing with Baillie's regulars, it must have been the Gordon foot under Colonel James Farquharson of Inverey, and

FERGUSON

*Irish swordsman, as depicted by McIan.*

Laghtnan and O'Cahan's Irish mercenaries who routed Leslie's Fife brigade. At any rate it was all over very quickly and the whole army completely disintegrated. Baillie and some of his officers tried to rally the fugitives at 'the brook', presumably where the A803 road crosses a stream at Auchincloch about two kilometres east of the battlefield, 'bot all in vaine.' Instead, the mounted officers retired to the Bridge of Denny and from there went their separate ways. Baillie and Holburne rode for Stirling where they were eventually joined by the cavalry, who were badly shaken but otherwise largely unscathed. Baillie's first instinct was to lead them south again into Clydesdale to rendezvous with another force led by the Earl of Lanark, but they flatly refused and so he set about securing Stirling with what remained of his infantry.

Surprisingly enough Baillie's regular infantry units must also have held together fairly well in the retreat and were consequently left well alone. All of them saw good service afterwards and even the 'three that were joyned in one' survived to be filled out again with new recruits and sent into England, but it was a very different story with the three Fife regiments. Dissolving into a panic-stricken rabble they were pursued for miles by the exultant clansmen and hundreds ruthlessly cut down.

In tactical terms the battle of Kilsyth on 15 August 1645 was just about as complete and decisive a victory as any general could wish for. Yet the battle's immediate aftermath presents a terrible anti-climax. In the first place the Royalists remained on or near the battlefield for another two days, which strongly argues that they too had been hard hit in the fighting. Then, once he did get the army moving again, Montrose passed up the opportunity to try and seize Stirling from Baillie's beaten army, but instead raided Glasgow before establishing a large camp at Bothwell, further up the Clyde. This served as a base for other raids, including one by Nathaniel Gordon on Edinburgh itself. He met no resistance there, save from the castle, and freed a number of Royalist prisoners, but he also brought back the dread news that the city was gripped by a Typhus epidemic. There could be no triumphant entry for the King's general.

The inactivity and the marauding proved just as destructive as a lost battle and the army was already disintegrating when on 2 or 3 September MacCholla left for good. He took 120 of the best of the Irish mercenaries, to serve as his lifeguard, and all the remaining Highlanders with him on his ultimately doomed attempt to re-establish MacDonald hegemony in the Western Isles. Seeking to legitimise his authority in the first flush of victory after Kilsyth, Montrose had summoned the Scots parliament to meet at Glasgow on 20 October, but now, realising that if he was to retain the initiative and above all aid his increasingly desperate King, Montrose bestirred himself into marching on Edinburgh after all, only for the Gordons to leave him as well after the first day's march.

He never reached the capital. Learning that the plague was still raging there, he instead turned south at Dalkeith on 6 September, optimistically hoping to make good his losses by raising large numbers of cavalry in the borders. He had certainly been promised support there by various local leaders including the Marquis of Douglas and the Earls of Home, Roxburgh and Traquair – though their best men had already been combed out for at least two successive levies for the government's own forces. The Marquis of Douglas at any rate joined him at Galashiels on 7 September with around 1,000 moss-troopers, but neither the Earl of Home nor the Earl of Roxburgh appeared at Kelso next day and although Traquair joined with a small troop, both he and his son left four days later, promising to raise more men. Nevertheless, untrained and undisciplined as these levies were it must have seemed to Montrose that he now had a respectable body of cavalry, far more than he had ever commanded before. By 10 September he was at Jedburgh, poised to move south into England when disturbing news reached him. Lieutenant General David Leslie had passed through Berwick on 6 September with at least four regiments of infantry and six regiments of cavalry.

Prudently, Montrose turned westwards, perhaps hoping to regain contact with MacCholla and the Gordons, but early on the morning of 14 September Leslie's troopers charged out of the mist and surprised the Royalists in their camp at Philiphaugh, just outside Selkirk. Leslie's victory was swift and decisive. Montrose barely escaped with his life, and a handful of his Irish mercenaries, but his little army was destroyed and although he tried to patch together another he never again posed a serious threat to the government and at the war's end slipped quietly abroad into exile, until summoned back for one last doomed campaign.

# *Dunbar*

Scottish intervention in the English Civil War brought about a Parliamentarian victory over the Cavaliers and that participation was bought by a substantial subsidy and the promise to reform the English Church according to the word of God. So far as the Scots were concerned that meant Presbyterianism and they were bitterly disappointed when their English colleagues placed a different interpretation on the scriptures at the war's end. In 1648 some of the more moderate Scots politicians entered into an 'Engagement' with the defeated King. This time the adoption of Presbyterianism was made explicit but the Scots invasion which followed met with disaster at Preston and cost King Charles I his head. A more hard line government then swept to power in Scotland with English backing, only to bewilder its allies by proclaiming his son as King Charles II at the Cross in Edinburgh.

Yet there was nothing inconsistent in this. As long ago as the Declaration of Arbroath the Scots had stoutly affirmed that the King reigned only by the consent of his people and now the return of young Charles was to be hedged about by all manner of conditions and restrictions. The negotiations were protracted and in an ill-fated attempt to improve his bargaining position Charles ordered the Marquis of Montrose to raise a rebellion in his name. It failed, Montrose was executed and with his bargaining position fatally undermined Charles sailed from Holland, duly signed the Covenant on 23 June and next day came ashore at Speymouth on the Scots government's terms.

No matter that the return of the king was to be hedged about by so many restraints as to reduce him to a mere figurehead, the very fact of his being allowed into the country at all confirmed English suspicions that the Scots still acknowledged his ultimate authority. It therefore followed, they feared, that sooner or later the Scots would invade England once again and seek to place their King on the throne at Westminster.

Accordingly, the English government resolved on a pre-emptive strike and on 22 July 1650 Oliver Cromwell crossed the border at Berwick with 16,354 men. Initially he met with no opposition, for until a month earlier the Scots army had numbered something in the region of only 2,500 horse and 3,000 foot. New levies had hurriedly been called out but the Scots commander, Alexander Leslie, Earl of Leven, knew it would take time to assemble and train them and so concentrated his forces at Edinburgh rather than on the border.

*Fifth Captain's colour, Colonel Charles Fairfax's Regiment of Foot. The Colonel's own colour was plain blue and, in 1649, he ordered that it 'must have (within a well wrought round) these two words (one under the other) "Fideliter Faeliciter", and a handsome compartment round about the word'.*

Unhindered by nothing more than bad roads Cromwell arrived in the small town of Dunbar four days later and it was not until 29 July that he at last discovered the main body of the Scots army dug in behind a line of forts and entrenchments stretching all the way from Edinburgh to Leith. There could be no question of mounting a formal frontal assault on this position, but, nevertheless, he rather optimistically tried to tempt the Scots to come out and fight. He placed his cavalry at Restalrig and his infantry at Jock's Lodge while four warships bombarded Leith. Leven refused to rise to the bait. Then to make matters worse, the weather turned bad. The English army spent the night in makeshift bivouacs under pouring rain and next morning 'the ground being very wet, and our provisions scarce' Cromwell decided to fall back on Musselburgh.

Discipline broke down almost at once. Cromwell, with the infantry, simply hurried down the road and soon left General Lambert and the rearguard dangerously exposed. Recognising an opportunity, the Scots cavalry emerged in pursuit. What followed was a severely chastening experience for the vaunted Ironsides. Some Scots who sallied out from Leith were quickly driven back by Colonel Hacker, but on the Edinburgh road it was a very different matter. Captain Evanson's troop of Whalley's Regiment, the rearmost unit, 'received the charge; but being overpowered by the enemy, retreated'. Cromwell's own regiment of Horse then charged forward to their rescue, but then more lancers came up and sent the Ironsides tumbling back in considerable confusion. Next Colonel Whalley counter-charged with four more troops of his regiment and Lambert also brought up his own regiment, only to become sucked into a fierce melee in which the greater weight of the English horses counted for nothing.

Lambert had his horse 'shot in the neck and head; himself run through the arm with a lance, and run through another part of his body', and was taken prisoner.

Couanant
for
Religion
King and
7
Kingdome

*Unidentified Scots Captain's colour with white saltire on blue (BM Harl. 1460/27). The red rose and figure 7 both denote the captain's seniority within the regiment.*

As he was being led off towards Edinburgh however Lieutenant Empson of Cromwell's Regiment charged and rescued him, and, shortly afterwards, having made their point, the Scots decided to call it a day.

Predictably enough Cromwell boasted of having 'killed divers of them upon the place, and took some prisoners, without any considerable loss' while the Scots equally optimistically claimed to have killed five colonels and lieutenant colonels, mortally wounded Lambert and 'above 500'. Nevertheless according to one of Cromwell's officers, his men eventually arrived at Musselburgh, 'so tired and wearied for want of sleep, and so dirty by reason of the weather, that we expected the enemy would make an infall upon us.' Worse was to follow. Indeed, that very night, the Scots followed up their success by mounting a heavy raid on the English camp.

In the early hours of the morning of 31 July Major General Robert Montgomerie attacked out of the darkness with as many as fifteen troops of horse numbering 800 or more picked cavalrymen, belonging to his own, Sir James Halkett's and Gibby Carr's regiments, and, according to at least one account, a couple of hundred infantry as well.

Montgomerie successfully achieved tactical surprise by posting a number of English Royalists at the head of his column. The familiar accents of these Cavaliers misled the outlying picquets into thinking that the approaching troopers were in fact a friendly patrol which was known to be out looking for the Scots. They realised their mistake too late and put up a fierce but all too brief resistance before the Scots charged into the camp, inflicting a number of casualties and spreading confusion, fear and despondency, before withdrawing just as quickly as they had come. On the way out, just by way of rounding off the excursion, Montgomerie's men ran into and dispersed the patrol they themselves had earlier been mistaken for!

Cromwell once again proclaimed the Scots' departure as a victory, but then at midnight on 5 August hastily pulled his army right back to Dunbar. The decision to withdraw was prompted in part by the rough weather which prevented any supplies being landed at Musselburgh, and by the difficulty in bringing them forward from Dunbar by road. Worse still, having gambled on good weather and a swift campaign, he had not brought tents for his men and they had suffered accordingly. The tents were at last landed at Dunbar but already the bad weather and scarcity of food was producing a very long sick list.

Nevertheless, Cromwell resolved on another attempt to bring the Scots to battle. This time he planned to swing around to the south and west of Edinburgh, along the line of the present City By-pass. It would mean cutting himself off from his base at Dunbar, but his aim was to re-establish contact with the fleet at Queensferry, to the west of Edinburgh. He would then have successfully interdicted the Scots' line of communications to Stirling and the west and would thus force them out into the open where he wanted them.

The move on Sunday, 13 August initially took the Scots by surprise, not least because it was the Lord's Day. However Cromwell could only carry three days' supplies so he initially seized a strong position on the Braid Hill in the Pentlands and then tried to enter into negotiations for a peaceful settlement. However although some of the Scots openly declared their detestation of the King they were not prepared to change sides.

With supplies running short Cromwell was soon compelled to fall back again to Musselburgh to pick up some more. In his absence the Scots promptly came out and occupied a strong blocking position on Corstorphine Hill. Hurrying back, Cromwell stormed a minor Scots outpost in a house at Redhall on 26 August but then decided that the Scots' main fighting position was far too strong, and so shifted further westwards once again in the hope of cutting the Scots lines of communication with Stirling. However the Earl of Leven, who was operating on interior lines, forestalled him again by blocking his path at the village of Gogar.

Cromwell immediately prepared to attack, only to call the operation off on realising that both of Leven's flanks were secured by boggy ground and that his invitingly open front was not only boggy as well but swept by artillery.

Unwilling to risk a battle under less than favourable conditions, unable to break through to the sea, short of supplies and increasingly concerned about his own line of communications, Cromwell once more fell back first to Musselburgh and then, on 31 August, pulled out for Dunbar. He rather disingenuously justified the move by expressing the hope that Leven might thereby be tempted to come out and fight, and in this at least he was not disappointed for at this point the Scots Army suddenly went over on to the offensive.

Throughout this period Leven and his second in command, Lieutenant General David Leslie had been working hard to improve the efficiency of their raw levies, both by 'exercising' them and by overseeing two successive purges of unsuitable officers. Notwithstanding a very widespread

## FENCIBLES

*The Scots army at Dunbar was still made up of conscripts raised under the long-established fencible system. By 1650 this mustering system, which was originally geared to sustain a single campaign, had been in more or less continuous operation for nearly twelve years and the government was reduced to exercising a very rudimentary rule of thumb in simply demanding a certain number of men to be levied from each sheriffdom. Unfortunately ordering the men to be levied out and actually mustering them into service were often two entirely different things. Some areas such as Fife and Kinross were fairly diligent in rounding up the required numbers, while others were much more backward. Unsurprisingly, Scots infantry regiments were almost invariably smaller than their English counterparts. On 25 June the Estates ordered the levying of some 9,749 foot and 2,882 horse, and a week later on 3 July 1650 a second levy was ordered which was even more optimistically expected to produce an additional 19,614 foot, forming twenty-one new infantry regiments. This second demand for men, following so soon after the first, largely proved to be counter-productive and once the 'old' regiments had been brought up to strength many of the new ones existed only as cadres.*

assumption, Lieutenant General David Leslie (d.1682) was neither Leven's nephew nor even a near kinsman, being instead a younger son of Sir Patrick Leslie of Pitcairlie in Fife and Lady Jean Stewart, a daughter of the Earl of Orkney. Leven by contrast was the illegitimate son of an Aberdeenshire laird, George Leslie of Balquhain and a 'wench in Rannoch'. Leven was a far better soldier than Leslie, but having been born in about 1580 was now too old for active campaigning. Nevertheless the two were confident enough to take the army out of its trenches not merely to pursue but to destroy the English army.

Cromwell, on the other hand, now showed no desire to stand and face them, but instead hurried straight for Haddington although quite inevitably his rearguard was beaten up in the process. It was thrown into disorder as it approached the town but fortunately 'the Lord by his providence put a cloud over the moon', and so the rear brigade of horse managed to break contact under cover of the resulting darkness. Nothing daunted, the Scots tried again at midnight and although details of the fight are lacking this must have been an altogether much more serious affair for it took an hour's fighting before they were repulsed by Colonel Charles Fairfax's Foot.

Next morning Cromwell drew up his exhausted army in order of battle, 'into an open field on the south side of Haddington' in the expectation that a battle was imminent. Whether the army was in much condition to withstand an attack is perhaps a moot point but 'having waited about the space of four hours to see if he would come to us and not finding any inclination in the enemy so to do, we resolved to go, according to our first intendment, to Dunbar'.

According to Cromwell this time the move went well:

By the time we had marched three or four miles, we saw some bodies of the enemie's horse draw out of their quarters; and by that time our carriages were gotten near Dunbar, their whole army was upon their march after us; and indeed our drawing back in this manner, with the addition of three new regiments added to them, did much heighten their confidence, if not presumption and arrogancy.

A Captain, John Hodgson, on the other hand, recalled the retreat rather differently and wrote how:

We staid until about ten o'clock, had been at prayer in several regiments, sent away our wagons and carriages towards Dunbar, and not long afterwards marched, a poor, shattered, hungry, discouraged army; and the Scots pursued very close, that our rearguard had much ado to secure our poor weak foot that was not able to march up. We drew near Dunbar towards night and the Scots ready to fall upon our rear: two guns played upon them, and so they drew off and left us that night, having got us unto a pound as they reckoned.

Cromwell drew up his army 'in battalia in the town fields, between the Scotch army and the town ready to engage.' The baggage train and the guns were at first secured in the churchyard but as night came on Cromwell drew the guns out again and placed them in the middle of his lines, no doubt expecting an attack early in the morning.

Instead, the greater part of Leven's army, instead of following on Cromwell's heels as he supposed, had slid eastwards. The previous night, while Cromwell's men were fighting off the attacks on the camp at Haddington, a Scots infantry brigade had been flung into the defile at Cockburnspath, cutting the Berwick road south of Dunbar. Now the bulk of the Scots army secured the commanding eminence of Doon Hill, overlooking Dunbar and the Berwick road. To all appearances Cromwell was now trapped.

However once the Scots were actually on top of Doon Hill it very soon became apparent – if indeed it had not been obvious from the very start – that the position suffered significant drawbacks and was no place to fight a battle.

The position certainly offered a magnificent view of the coastal plain and the English army below, and its steep slopes were undoubtedly unassailable, but those advantages counted for nothing if the English would not oblige with an attack. On the other had, so long as the Scots remained on top of the hill there was very little they could do to hinder or impede the movements of the English, particularly since they had few heavy guns. What was more, the bad weather was now turning much worse. The hill-top offered no shelter from either wind or rain and it is significant that in the immediate aftermath of the battle Cromwell released a large number of 'sick' Scots captives who were undoubtedly suffering from exposure.

Although masterminding the campaign Leven had apparently remained behind in Edinburgh, and it was his deputy, David Leslie, who now undertook to descend the hill not to engage the English in a battle of annihilation, but to merely to properly block the Berwick road. Indeed, as the Reverend Robert Baillie recorded, the subsequent inquiry into the conduct of David Leslie concluded that he was guilty of

> no maladministration... but the removall of the armie from the hill the night before the rowt, which yet was a consequence of the Committee's order, contrare to his mind, to stop the enemie's retreat, and for that end storm Broxmouth House so soon as possible.

Of itself this decision was quite sensible, but although the move began shortly before sunrise on 2 September it was not until about four in the afternoon that the artillery and baggage was finally brought down and secured beside Meikle Pinkerton farm. The length and difficulty of the operation once again emphasising the impracticality of the original hill-top position.

In the meantime, Cromwell brought his own army forward from Dunbar and formed a battle-line on the north side of the Broxburn. Leslie, no doubt wary of being attacked before his men were properly deployed, conformed by arranging his own battle line along the southern side. The Broxburn, although neither particularly deep nor broad, mostly runs through a broad trench-like ravine and constitutes a significant military obstacle, particularly since the northern or Dunbar side of the ravine is rather higher than the southern side and very largely dominates it.

Between the Berwick road (A1) and the sea on the other hand it is much easier to cross the stream and as Baillie noted, Leslie had designs upon the main crossing point near Broxmouth House. There was some skirmishing during the latter part of the afternoon, since Cromwell was equally alive to its importance and at one stage a particularly vicious fight took place for possession of a minor crossing point at what is now Brand's Mill:

> On the side of the bank was a poor house which stood in a shelving pass; Lieut.-Gen. Fleetwood and Col. Pride sent 24 foot and 6 horse to secure that pass, that the enemy should not come over. The enemy about four of the clock drew down about two troops of lanciers into this pass to beat off the said party; the six horse gave way; they killed 3 of the foot and took 3, and wounded and drove away the rest, and so they gained the pass, but nevertheless kept it not.

This seemingly pointless skirmish was presumably intended to cover a partial deployment of the Scots army for Leslie rather belatedly realised that having lined up opposite the English army, he was actually positioned in the wrong place. Accordingly he now tried to extend his right towards the sea, and Cromwell noted the movement of about two thirds of the Scots horse from the left flank to reinforce the right, which took place shortly after the skirmish at Brand's Mill. Otherwise Leslie's redeployment was hampered by the very restricted space between the Broxburn and the foot of the hill and by nightfall on 2 September most of his infantry were still positioned to the left of the Berwick road with the all but impassable ravine directly to their front.

Notwithstanding the unsatisfactory deployment, Leslie had firmly blocked the Berwick road. Cromwell knew he was in trouble and called a council of war.

There is little doubt that by the evening of 2 September the 'poor, shattered, hungry, discouraged' English army was pretty well at the end of its tether. Captain Hodgson, although not present at the council of war reckoned that; 'Many of the colonels were for shipping the foot, and the horse to force the passage'. Instead, according to Hodgson, Major General Lambert forcefully, if not inspirationally, advocated an all-out assault with the object of turning Leslie's right, pinning the Scots army against the slopes of Doon Hill and then destroying it. On the other hand a soldier turned artist and hack writer named Fitzpayne Fisher quite unwittingly reveals that the council of war almost certainly produced a rather different resolution and that the 'opportunity' was not the destruction of the Scots army.

When the English army arrived in Dunbar on 1 September the baggage train was secured within the walled churchyard beyond the eastern end of the town. Yet Fisher's contemporary picture map of the battle, prepared from eyewitness testimony

*Blue cavalry cornet belonging to the Master of Forbes' Horse.*

PVGNA
PRO
PATRIA

NEC TEMERE

NEC TIMIDE

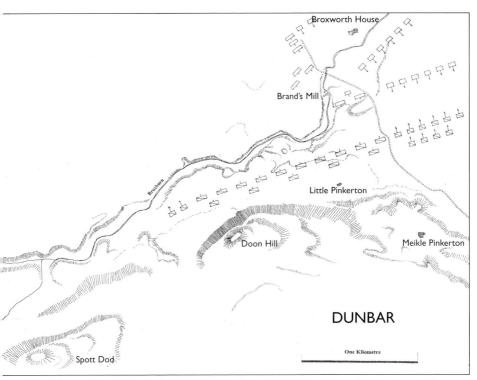

*Dispositions at dawn. Monck's infantry brigade and most of the English cavalry have crossed the Broxburn and are about to attack the Scots right wing in order to force open the Berwick road.*

for a proposed official history of the campaign, shows both the churchyard and the adjacent English camp to be empty. Instead the baggage train is clearly and unambiguously placed within the grounds of Broxmouth House – Cromwell's tactical headquarters and the jumping off point for the assault.

Obviously therefore the attack at dawn next morning was not the outcome of a bold resolution to go forward and fight the enemy, but a desperate attempt to force open the Berwick road in order that the army could cut its way out of the trap and escape southwards. The baggage train had all-too evidently been brought up to the forefront of the army in order that once the withdrawal commenced it could be passed down the road as soon as possible rather than left to become entangled with the rearguard.

This in turn no doubt explains why Cromwell, 'rid all the night before through the several regiments by torchlight, upon a little Scots nag, biting his lip till the blood ran down his chin without his perceiving it, his thoughts being busily employed to be ready for the action now at hand'. There was little wonder he was nervous, for having declined the option of trying to evacuate at least a part of his army by sea he now gambling everything on re-opening the road and escaping overland. If the dawn attack failed the army would have little alternative but to surrender.

Under cover of darkness the English army was pulled out of its battle-line along

*Doon Hill as seen from the English position.*

the Broxburn and assembled astride the Berwick road, one brigade stacked behind the other in readiness for the breakout. The Scots army seems to have been aware that something was happening for it too remained standing to its arms for much of the wet and windy night and at 'ten o'clock the enemy did give an alarm to ours. The whole army then being in a readiness they were repulsed'. This was probably no more than a demonstration and after it was over the Scots began to settle down. At about midnight Major General Holburne gave permission for all but two musketeers in each company to extinguish their slow-match. Ordinarily this would have been a sensible enough precaution which not only prevented waste and

*Dunbar as seen from the top of Doon Hill. The line of the Broxburn can be seen very clearly, as can the way in which the northern bank, where Cromwell first drew up his forces, completely dominates the southern bank.*

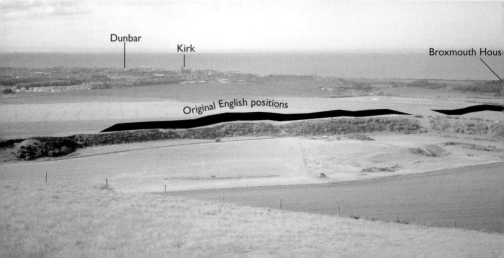

ensured that the match could be kept dry within the soldiers' clothing - but also meant that the soldiers themselves could try to snatch some sleep.

As the soldiers 'made themselves shelter of the corn new-reapt,' many of the cavalrymen and officers retired to their tents and Leslie complained two days after the battle that 'I know I get my share of the salt for drawing them so near the enemy, and must suffer in this as many times formerly; though I take God to witness we might as easily have beaten them as we did James Graham at Philiphaugh, if the officers had stayed by their own troops and regiments'. Thus they were quite unprepared when, at about four in the morning, General Fleetwood moved forward to secure the crossing points over the Broxburn.

Cromwell afterwards reckoned that after allowing for his many sick, he had 7,500 infantry and 3,500 cavalry fit to fight at Dunbar on the morning of 3 September. His leading brigade was commanded by John Lambert and comprised Fleetwood's, Lambert's and Whalley's regiments of Horse. Immediately behind was another cavalry brigade made up of Lilburne's, Hacker's and Twisleton's regiments, almost certainly commanded by Colonel Robert Lilburne. Assuming Cromwell's estimate to be correct, the two brigades presumably mustered about 1,500 men apiece. Next came Colonel George Monck's rather weak infantry brigade comprising his own and Malverer's regiments, and five companies of Colonel George Fenwick's, probably totalling something in the region of about 2,000 men. Cromwell's official report on the battle rather perfunctorily implies that Lieutenant General Fleetwood was in overall charge of this 'vanguard', though Lambert was actually to play a leading role in the coming fight.

Next came two more infantry brigades. Colonel Thomas Pride's Brigade was made up of his own regiment together with the Lord General's, under Major Goffe, and Major General Lambert's. Behind Pride's was Colonel Robert Overton's Brigade. His own regiment was not present, but he did have those of Coxe, Daniel and Charles Fairfax. Each of the brigades must have had about 2,500 men Finally in the rear of all came Cromwell's own regiment of Horse acting as a reserve. His official despatch however actually refers to the two regiments in the reserve, which presumably means that his regiment was brigaded with two companies of Okey's Dragoons who were equipped as Horse.

This then was the force assigned to destroy the Scots right wing and re-open the Berwick road. As to the rest it would appear that the mounted infantry element of Okey's Dragoons still maintained a picquet line along the edge of the Broxburn while the artillery was in all probability placed on the high ground above Brand's Mill where, as Lambert recommended they 'might have fair play at their left wing while we were fighting their right'.

On the other side of the Broxburn information on the Scots dispositions remains scanty. The majority of the Scots cavalry, numbering about 2,500 troopers, were on the right wing and largely posted between the Berwick road and the sea-shore. The first line should have been commanded by Major General Robert Montgomerie, while the second is known to have been led by Colonel Archibald Strachan. No more than a single brigade remained on the left wing and the only unit which can be identified there is Colonel William Stewart's – he may well have been the brigade commander.

*Cavalry fight as depicted by John Cruso c.1632.*

As to the infantry, the five brigades identified in an English intelligence summary (BM Harl.6844) can be placed with rather more confidence. As the senior infantry commander, Sir James Lumsden had his brigade on the extreme right by the Berwick road. As next in seniority, Major General James Holburne's Brigade will by convention have stood on the extreme left, while the third major general, Colin Pitscottie, had the centre. There is ample evidence that Sir James Campbell of Lawers' Brigade was posted on the right between Lumsden's and Pitscottie's men, which leaves Colonel John Innes' Brigade standing between Pitscottie's and Holburne's.

Sir James Lumsden's brigade was at least a fairly strong one, comprising the General of the Artillery's Regiment, Sir William Douglas of Kirkness' Regiment and his own, and mustering over 2,000 men at the outset of the campaign. Unfortunately although long-standing custom in all armies placed the brigade on the right it was unique it being entirely made up of new recruits. Lawers' brigade made up of his own, Sir George Preston of Valleyfield's and Sir John Haldane of Gleneagles' regiments had about the same number. Pitscottie's, which included a composite battalion of Borderers under Sir David Home of Wedderburn, and Colonel John Lindsay of Edzell's Regiment, had only about 1,600 in total. Colonel John Innes' Brigade, which came down from the north and comprised his own and Colonel John Forbes of Leslie's regiments as well as element's of Lovat's and Argyle's was even weaker and probably only had something between 1,200 and 1,500, although Major General Holburne's Brigade, made up of Sir George Buchannan of Buchannan's, Holburne's, and Colonel Alexander Stewart's regiments must have had around 2,000 men.

In total the Scots infantry may have mustered as many as 9,500 men, rather than the 16,000 claimed by Cromwell, although it has to be stressed that this estimate does not allow for wastage. In any case any slight advantage in numbers which might have existed was to be compromised both by Leslie's faulty dispositions and above all by the trick of fate which placed his rawest brigade squarely in the path of the English breakout.

*Little Pinkerton Farm (and the cement works) from Doon Hill. Cromwell's initial crossing and the cavalry battle took place in the middle distance between Little Pinkerton and the sea. Much of the area has been quarried away.*

*Fully equipped musketeer as depicted in Jacob de Gehyn's* Exercise of Arms.

At about four in the morning Cromwell's men moved forward to secure the crossing points over the Broxburn. Lambert's cavalry brigade immediately ran into the Scottish picquet line and drove them back on their supports, but there the attack stalled until Monck came up with his infantry brigade and a furious fire-fight began. The semi-official True Relation describes how

A party of ours, advancing to gain the wind of the enemy, were discovered by a party of theirs who came to alarm us; but notwithstanding (through the Lord's great mercy), after above an hours dispute at the pass upon the broadway between Dunbar and Berwick, our men obtained their end, possessed the pass, whereby we might with ease come over with our army.

One account reported that they fought for a time by moonlight, but after about an hour both sides gave over and waited for first light which came around 5.30.

For the Scots it should have been an opportunity to re-group, but as Leslie complained, far too many officers were absent and although he implied that it was regimental officers who were missing, they also included many of the senior officers. It is significant that the authorisation to extinguish the musketeers' slow-match was given by Holburne, who was only a brigade commander. At any rate when the fighting resumed after about half an hour Lambert scattered the first line of Scots cavalry and even got in amongst their tents before being driven back by a series of counter-attacks led not by Major General Montgomerie, but by Colonel Archibald Strachan.

In the meantime Colonel Monck crashed into Lumsden's Brigade on the right of the Scots infantry. Despite the fact that they must already have been engaged when the Broxburn crossings were seized an hour earlier Lumsden's men were evidently unprepared for the onslaught. The brigade disintegrated immediately. Lumsden was badly wounded and captured and Douglas of Kirkness was killed, as was Lieutenant Colonel David Wemyss, the commander of the General of the Artillery's Regiment. A large number of colours can be identified as having been taken from the brigade and afterwards the General of the Artillery's was the only regiment to be reconstituted.

Nevertheless the fight was not entirely one-sided, for Lumsden and his men managed to hold on just long enough for Campbell of Lawers' Brigade to counter-attack and knock Monck's Brigade out of the fight. At the same time Colonel Strachan rallied the second line of the Scots cavalry and likewise flung Lambert back across the Broxburn. Cromwell's breakout attempt must have seemed in jeopardy,

*The area between Little Pinkerton and the Broxburn where Lawers' brigade made its stand. Note the steep northern slope of Doon Hill which hampered Scots efforts to redeploy.*

but he persevered and now committed Colonel Thomas Pride's infantry brigade:

> our first foot after they had discharged their duty (being overpowered with the enemy), received some repulse, which they soon recovered. But my own regiment, under the command of Lieutenant Colonel Goffe, and my major, White, did seasonably come in; and, at push of pike, did repel the stoutest regiment the enemy had there.

The attack was obviously a hasty one for Pride's Brigade seems to have engaged piecemeal. The True Relation states that 'The Lord General's regiment of foot charged the enemy with much resolution, and were seconded by Colonel Pride's, while Lambert's Foot scarcely got into the fight at all. According to Hodgson, then a captain in the regiment 'The General himself comes in the rear of our regiment and commands to incline to the left; that was, to take more ground to be clear of all bodies'. As a result the regiment became bogged down in petty skirmishing with 'straggling parties' by Little Pinkerton – presumably the remnants of Lumsden's Brigade.

Meanwhile, Lambert brought Robert Lilburne's cavalry brigade forward from the second line and charged Strachan in front, while Cromwell's own regiment of Horse led by Captain Packer, having crossed the Broxburn down by the sea-shore, charged him in flank. This time the Scots cavalry were completely routed.

Instead of pursuing them, Cromwell and Lambert now halted to decide what to do next. Traditionally their troopers are said to have sung the 117th Psalm; *Oh Give you praise unto the Lord* while they waited and it must have been now rather than on the night before that Cromwell took the decision to encompass the total defeat of the Scots army instead of merely trying to break out.

The cramped nature of the battlefield was causing problems for both sides by this time. Monck's Brigade was still out of action and it was proving difficult for Overton's to get into the fight effectively, but the Scots were in a much worse position, hemmed in between the Broxburn and the base of Doon Hill. As the sun rose Cromwell seized his opportunity, pushing his cavalry around the right flank of Lawers' position and into the rear of the Scots infantry.

*The Scots army tried to escape across this area below Doon Hill, but many were captured on the sands of Belhaven Bay, just to the right of centre.*

Haddington     Edinburgh     Belhaven Bay

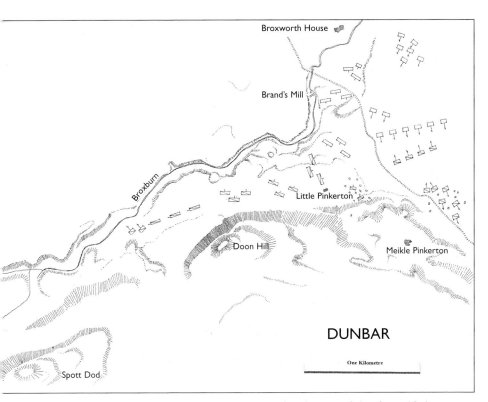

*The Scots' right wing is collapsing. The Scots' front line cavalry have been routed. Strachan, with the second line has thrown Lambert back but is about to be attacked by the English second line. Lumsden's infantry brigade has been destroyed, but the situation is temporarily stabilised by Lawer's brigade, drawn up between Little Pinkerton and the Broxburn. Monck's brigade has been repulsed but Pride's and Overton's are moving up, supported by Cromwell's own regiment of horse. Further to the west some Scots units are already starting to withdraw.*

So far Lawers' men had been holding their own and Gumble, in his well known Life of Monck, describes how

> Onely Lawers his regiment of Highlanders made a good defence, and the chief officer, a lieutenant colonell, being slain by one of the general's sergeants (the colonel was absent), of the name of the Campbells, they stood to the push of pike and were all cut in pieces.

They must indeed have 'stood' it pretty well, for another English commentator related how the Scots 'would not yield though at push of pike and butt-end of musket until a troop of horse charged from one end to another of them, and so left them to the mercy of the foot'.

The destruction of this regiment appeared, to an elated Cromwell and his officers, to precipitate a total collapse of Scottish resistance. One reported that

> Our horse immediately rallying and our foot advancing charged the enemy, and put them to the run very suddenly, it being near six o'clock of the morning.

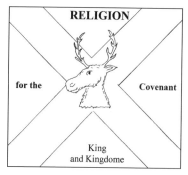

RELIGION

for the                    Covenant

King
and Kingdome

*Unknown captain's colour from Colonel John Forbes of Leslie's Regiment: yellow saltire on green with stag's head proper – probably a Captain Forbes (BM Harl. 1460/75).*

Which rout the enemy's foot seeing, threw down their arms and fled.

The few surviving Scots accounts are even briefer, but nevertheless it is possible to build up a fairly detailed picture of this last phase of the battle as the Scots infantry struggled to reach safety.

Surprisingly enough the 'battalia which stood very stiffly to it' was probably not Campbell of Lawers' Regiment at all, but Sir John Haldane of Gleneagles'. Haldane himself was certainly killed, together with his lieutenant colonel, Robert Melvill, and Major John Cockburn, and the regiment was never reconstituted. Yet the other two regiments in the brigade, Lawers' and Valleyfield's, both escaped and, with the addition of a new regiment raised by Sir James Wood of Balbegno, the brigade was fit to take the field again by the end of the year.

Gleneagles' Regiment must have stood and fought so hard because it was serving as a rearguard, which indicates that Leslie may already have been trying to withdraw when Cromwell launched the decisive attack. As if by way of confirmation Fisher's useful picture-map of the battlefield depicts the attempted retreat not of a mob of fugitives but of formed bodies of Scots infantry.

Exactly the same experience was repeated with Pitscottie's Brigade. In order to escape, Leslie and Holburne first had to get their men across the Broxburn and the only practical place to do this was on the far left at what is now Doon Bridge. Holburne's and Innes's brigades and perhaps a part of Pitscottie's Brigade may have got across safely, but Wedderburn's combined battalion of Borderers was not so lucky, and like Gleneagles' men, may have down fighting to give the rest of the brigade time to cross.

Indeed one Scots account explicitly states that; 'Two regiments of foot fought it out manfully, for they were all killed as they stood (as the enemy confessed)'. While it is possible that the two regiments fought side by side, the evidence indicates that they actually fought in two quite separate actions.

Gleneagles' men certainly fought and died alone while Lawers' and Valleyfield's regiments escaped. Now Wedderburn was killed, together with both his son, Lieutenant Colonel George Home, and Lieutenant Colonel James Ker. Sir James Douglas of Mouswall and a Major William Menzies appear to have been the only field officers from the composite regiment to escape and a particularly large number of colours was also taken from the unit. Once again however both of the other regiments in the brigade, Pitscottie's and Edzell's, escaped more or less intact.

Having crossed the Broxburn the surviving Scots' infantry then marched hard for Haddington, but their retreat was harried all the way by the English cavalry and even some infantry in what must have been a long drawn out running battle.

Unsurprisingly, Colonel John Innes' little brigade was badly cut up in the retreat, but although he lost his lieutenant colonel, both his own regiment and the combined Highland battalion under Lovat survived to be rebuilt again in their old garrisons. Forbes of Leslie's Regiment on the other hand certainly disintegrated, but while it lost most of its colours it does not actually seem to have lost many officers or men. As for Holburne, the evidence suggests that he too got most of his brigade away intact, although Colonel Alexander Stewart was killed and his regiment completely destroyed, losing all its colours – perhaps in another forlorn rearguard action.

Most of the prisoners and the colours were taken during this final stage of the battle, as some regiments threw down their arms and scattered. Some fugitives, according to both Hodgson and Gumble, actually fled towards Dunbar and were taken on the sands at Belhaven, but most held on their course for twelve terrible kilometres until they reached Haddington. There the pursuit ended although Hacker's Regiment followed them a little further just to make sure.

Cromwell boasted at the time of having slain 3,000 Scots 'upon the place or near it' and taking as many as 10,000 prisoners, which exceeds the total number of Scots present at the battle. Balfour, while admitting that many of the foot were taken prisoner, noted in his journal that there were '8 or 900 killed'. This is borne out by reports that Leslie was falling back on Stirling with 4-5,000 men, at least half of whom must have been formed bodies of infantry.

On the other hand, Cromwell only admitted to some thirty to forty killed and moved swiftly to follow up his victory. Next day Lambert was sent forward to Edinburgh with a regiment of infantry and all of the cavalry except Hacker's Regiment, which was assigned the job of escorting the prisoners southwards. Having cleared the battlefield, Cromwell followed him with the rest of the army two days later. Edinburgh was surrendered without a fight on 7 September, but by that time Leslie had fallen back to Stirling. Intent on finishing him off, Cromwell followed, but hampered by 'extraordinary wet and stormy' weather and bad roads he did not arrive there until 17 September.

In the meantime as the English approached Leslie threw himself into the task of reconstituting his shattered forces. Three of his five infantry brigades had escaped from Dunbar battered but more or less intact and to them were added those levies who had either not reached the army in time to fight, or who had been left behind as insufficiently trained or equipped. It was very much a scratch force, many were 'green new levied sojours' and Stirling was 'not yet fortified as it should be', but it was enough.

Cromwell duly summoned the town on the morning of 18 September, but the Scots were unimpressed; no-one in the English army had the stomach for an assault and he was just going through the motions. Even in their incomplete state the defences were too strong for a frontal assault and the position could not be outflanked. Next day the English fell back again to Linlithgow and, having established a strong garrison there Cromwell himself retired all the way back to Edinburgh. It would be a year later before the final reckoning came with the Scots army at Worcester.

# Inverkeithing

For the next ten months Linlithgow Bridge and the river Avon would form the northern frontier of English-occupied Scotland, but of immediate English concern was the siege of Edinburgh Castle. Despite its having been rather unexpectedly stormed by a handful of men under Alexander Leslie and Sandie Hamilton back at the beginning of the Civil wars in 1639, it was generally regarded as impregnable and the siege was no more than a blockade. Nevertheless, the governor, Walter Dundas, was equally unenthusiastic – having to put up with the numerous kirkmen who took refuge there after Dunbar must have been a sore trial – and the castle's defiance was more symbolic than real. For a time a far more serious threat was posed by a new army being gathered in the west by Gibby Kev and Archibald Strachan, and by the rise of the Moss Troopers.

Kev at least was soon dealt with. Major General Lambert was sent after him with most of the cavalry, only to be unexpectedly attacked in his quarters at Hamilton in the early hours of 1 December 1650. Very literally caught napping, Lambert was quickly driven out of the town but in the process Kev's troopers themselves fell into some disorder and when he ordered them back out of the burgh to reorganise in the open, the raw levies jumped to the conclusion he was retreating and began to run. A greatly relieved Lambert then charged forward again, completed the accidental rout and captured Kev into the bargain. Later that day Cromwell himself moved on Glasgow whilst Strachan, whose loyalty had long been compromised by his conscience, disbanded his men and defected to the English.

Dealing with the Moss Troopers or 'Mossers' was far more difficult. At first they had simply been a nuisance; roving bands of fugitives turned bandits, but in time they developed into a real threat. The most notorious of the bands was led by a 'heigh German' mercenary known as Captain Augustine, and on the night of 13 December he crossed the Forth at Blackness with 120 men and made his way to Edinburgh. Swinging his way around to the far side he got in through the Canongate Port by the tried and trusted method of placing an English trooper at the head of the column. Once inside the Mossers then simply galloped straight up the High Street, deposited, by

## MOSS TROOPERS

*The term 'Moss trooper' is often, but quite erroneously applied to the Anglo-Scots border reiver of the sixteenth century. In fact there was an important difference between them in that most border reivers were otherwise respectable farmers and landowners, who from time to time set forth from their castles to steal livestock from their neighbours - ideally but not invariably on the other side of the border. Moss troopers on the other hand were landless bandits, usually operating in wandering gangs, lurking in the mosses and maintaining themselves by highway robbery and petty thievery as well as cattle rustling. Initially the moss troopers who preyed on Cromwell's stragglers and despatch riders were just such bandits. But once they began to be organised under the command of regular officers such as Augustine (probably Captain Augustine Hoffman, formerly of Leslie's Horse), and Patrick Gordon, alias 'Steilhand the Mosser', they developed into first-class light cavalry.*

way of supplies, a quantity of ammunition and pickling spices in the castle, then burst out again half an hour later and got clean away. The castle still surrendered ten days later, but the raid was a clear sign that the Scots were regaining their confidence.

Ironically enough, although Cromwell had gained an outstanding tactical victory at Dunbar, he had completely failed to achieve his primary political objective of neutralising the supposed threat posed by Charles Stuart. On the contrary, the net effect of Dunbar was to discredit the hitherto dominant Kirk party and so strengthen the position of the King and the increasingly militant Royalist party.

Astonishingly this resurgence of Royalist support actually resulted a brief civil war in the unoccupied part of Scotland. On 4 October the Earl of Atholl openly declared for the King and Charles slipped away from his semi-confinement in an attempt to reach him, only to be apprehended by Leslie in Glen Clova next day. Undaunted, Major General John Middleton also declared for the King shortly afterwards and began mustering substantial forces, including a fair number of regulars with whom he attacked and defeated Sir John Browne in a vicious skirmish at Newtyle in Forfarshire on 21 October 1650. One of Browne's officers and fifteen troopers were killed, and 120 taken prisoner. Significantly nearly half of Browne's men then changed sides and joined the Royalists, but when Leslie was ordered north to deal with the rebels they fell back to the Marquis of Huntly's castle at Strathbogie. There common sense reasserted itself and they agreed to disband their forces on 4 November. A month later however the balance of power changed dramatically and decisively with the defeat of Ker, and Strachan's defection to the English. Sensing the way the wind was going Leslie re-aligned himself with the Royalists and on 1 January 1651 Charles II was at last formally crowned at Scone, outside Perth.

This roused Cromwell to lead another push against Stirling in early February, but although Leslie was forced to evacuate his outpost at Callendar House and

*The Scots' left as seen from Lambert's position on the Ferry Hills. Once again the damage caused by heroic engineering is apparent.*

Ferry Hills

*The Scots right wing, including Duart's and Buchannan's regiments, were drawn up here on the forward slopes of Castland Hill. There is no mention of the knoll in the centre being wooded at the time of the battle. In the left distance can be seen the Ferry Hills where Lambert's men were posted. Even in this photograph the extent of the damage caused by road building is all too obvious.*

covered the withdrawal with a skirmish on the Carse of Balquiderock, where Bruce had triumphed so long ago, the English army again halted and then fell back to Edinburgh in appalling weather. This time Cromwell himself fell ill and was effectively laid up until June.

In the meantime the Scots recovery went on apace as a new and increasingly confident field army came together at Stirling. Linlithgow had already been raided once in January and on 14 April a large party of horse and dragoons, probably led by Augustine, (who now had a colonel's commission) mounted another much more successful raid:

> taking advantage of an exceeding misty and foggy morning, fell with their horse into Lithgow; they killd only one man, hastned out again: but the major [John Sydenham] with about 30 horse went forth of the town, giving order for the rest to follow. As soon as he was drawn forth, the enemy charged him, and he brake in among them; but his men forsaking him, the enemy pursued both him and them to the town, cutting and hacking them. A fresh party of ours being recollected, the enemy forthwith retreated, and were pursued; in the pursuit our men took 2 or 3 of theirs prisoners, and about 2 or 3 of ours were slain.

In fact the English were far more badly beaten than they first admitted, for not only did Major Sydenham die of his wounds, but a Captain Dowson and eight of his men were captured and then murdered by the Mossers.

The raid was soon followed by a more substantial move back into the South West, which forced the English to evacuate Hamilton. On 19 May Major General Robert Montgomerie won a neat little victory at Paisley. At much the same time

Middleton, having reassembled his Royalist forces brought them in to the camp at Stirling and thus reinforced, Leslie essayed a push southwards into the Torwood at the end of June. Cromwell duly came up from Edinburgh to meet him, only for the Scots to take up a strong position behind the river Carron. In a vain attempt to lure Leslie out of this position Cromwell first laid siege to Callendar House and then stormed it, slaughtering the governor, Lieutenant Galbraith and all sixty of his garrison. Despite this provocation Leslie refused to budge and eventually retired again into the defences of Stirling. Baffled, Cromwell cast about for a means of outflanking him.

Back in January Colonel Monck had unsuccessfully attempted a landing at Burntisland on the north shore of the Firth of Forth, but was thwarted by contrary winds. Now, after an abortive attempt to locate a suitable ford above Stirling, Cromwell decided to try another landing, with a much larger force, and early on the morning of 17 July 1651 while the greater part of his army ostentatiously demonstrated in front of Stirling, he embarked:

> Colonel [William] Daniel's regiment of foot, with as many forth of Leith as made them sixteen hundred with four troops of Colonel Lidcot's regiment, all commanded by Colonel [Robert] Overton. And accordingly attempted landing at Queen's Ferry, where almost on three sides the sea encompasseth a rocky piece of ground, which, with the loss of about six men, was effected... this done they presently fell to intrenching themselves.

The move was not unexpected. For some time the Scots had been building up the garrison of nearby Burntisland with fresh levies under a veteran officer, Colonel Harie Barclay and he evidently had an outpost at North Queensferry. Not only were Overton's men shot up as they landed but word was passed back to Stirling so swiftly that notwithstanding Cromwell's demonstration, Sir John Browne and Major General James Holburne were immediately sent off with their brigades of cavalry and infantry. In the meantime, as Major General Lambert reported, a tense stand-off escalated as those Scots units already quartered in the immediate vicinity turned up, and more English units were shipped across.

The enemy received the alarm the same day about ten of the clock, and sent a considerable party of horse and foot to beat ours back, upon which my lord [Cromwell] had some thoughts of attempting the enemy where they lay, which was not thought fit, but resolved to the contrary; and, in order to the preservation of the forces, his lordship commanded me to march hither with two regiments of horse and two of foot.

Upon Saturday, very early, we came to the water-side, and though I made all possible speed to boat over it, I could not get over more than the foot and my own regiment of horse all that day and the next night: about four in the afternoon on Saturday I discovered the enemy's body advanced as far as Dumfermling, within five miles of us, being, to my judgement, about four thousand.

And that night they encamped there, and, it seems, hearing more forces were come over, got a recruit of five hundred men the next day. All Saturday night we laboured to get over our horse, and before the last came to shore on the Lord's day, the enemy was advanced very near us.

By this time Lambert had in total; his own and Colonel William Daniel's Foot, reinforced by four companies of Colonel George Fenwick's; Colonel Francis West's Foot and Colonel Edmund Syler's Foot; his own regiment of Horse; Colonel John Okey's former dragoons; and Colonel Leonard Lytcott's Horse. The quality of this force seems to have been a little questionable. His own regiment of Foot was certainly a good one, but Daniel's had only been raised the year before, originally for service in Ireland, and had been left in reserve at Dunbar. Nothing is known of West's Regiment other than it was disbanded a year or two later, while Syler's may have been a militia regiment from Lincolnshire. As to the cavalry, both Lambert's and Okey's regiments were good veteran ones, but Lytcott's were also newly raised and would perform badly in the coming fight. It is hard to escape the impression that it was very largely a scratch force thrown together from second-line units.

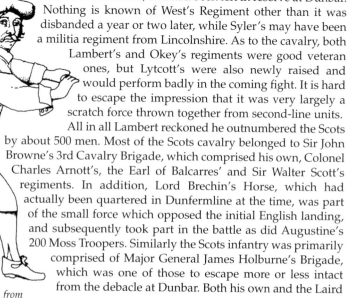

All in all Lambert reckoned he outnumbered the Scots by about 500 men. Most of the Scots cavalry belonged to Sir John Browne's 3rd Cavalry Brigade, which comprised his own, Colonel Charles Arnott's, the Earl of Balcarres' and Sir Walter Scott's regiments. In addition, Lord Brechin's Horse, which had actually been quartered in Dunfermline at the time, was part of the small force which opposed the initial English landing, and subsequently took part in the battle as did Augustine's 200 Moss Troopers. Similarly the Scots infantry was primarily comprised of Major General James Holburne's Brigade, which was one of those to escape more or less intact from the debacle at Dunbar. Both his own and the Laird

*Ordinary Scots soldier, from a contemporary print.*

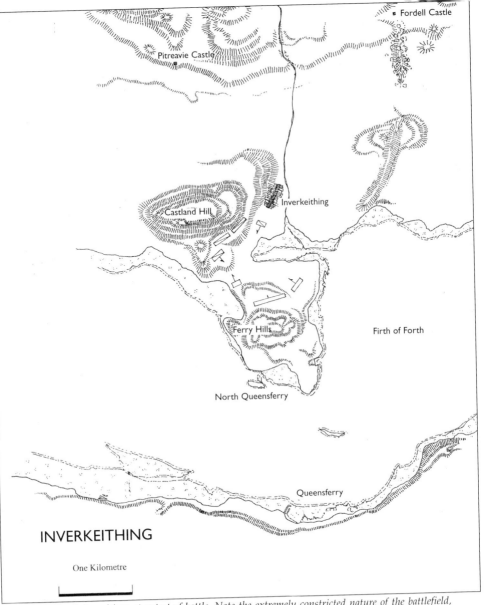

■ Fordell Castle

Pitreavie Castle

Inverkeithing

Castland Hill

Ferry Hills

Firth of Forth

North Queensferry

Queensferry

# INVERKEITHING

One Kilometre

*Conjectural dispositions at outset of battle. Note the extremely constricted nature of the battlefield, hampering more conventional deployment.*

of Buchannan's regiments were quite large, mustering 646 and 896 men respectively on 18 July. Stewart's Regiment, destroyed at Dunbar, had since been replaced by the Master of Grey's, 610 strong, which will have given Holburne a total of 2,152 regular infantry, exclusive of officers. The 'recruit of 500 men' which Lambert reported to have arrived on the Sunday morning was presumably the regiment of Highland clansmen led by Sir Hector MacLean of Duart which was to figure so prominently in the battle. One account of the affair credits the Scots with having five regiments of foot and it is likely that the otherwise unidentified fifth unit was a detachment of Barclay's men from Burntisland, but there is no indication of their number.

Both armies drew up facing each other, the English on the Ferry Hills and Scots on the lower slopes of Castland Hill, with their right anchored on Whinney Hill and their left on the Hill of Selvege, or Muckle Hill, a little to the south of Inverkeithing. Some of them may have been dug in, for Lambert afterwards spoke of burying some of the Scots dead in their trenches.

On the one hand Holburne was understandably leery of assaulting the strong English position with a single brigade of infantry, while Lambert had no intention of going anywhere until he had brought across all his troops. However the arrival of the last of Okey's Horse was the signal for Holburne, who by now was outnumbered, to order a withdrawal.

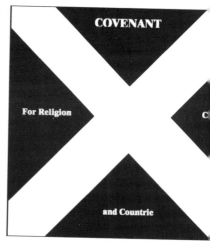

*Typical Scots infantry colour of the period Shortly before Inverkeithing a Scots Royalist officer said he hoped 'to see the word on their colors to be Covenant for tobacco, strong water and whores'.*

In his report Lambert described how Holburne 'began to wheel, as if he meant either to march away, or take the advantage of a steep mountain'. The 'mountain' was of course Castland Hill and this indicates that Holburne, having originally been facing south, was now wheeling backwards, preparatory to retiring on Dunfermline. Sensing he might have them on the run Lambert immediately sent forward Okey's Regiment to engage the Scots rearguard, whereupon Holburne halted again and drew up his men in order of battle.

Duart's Highland regiment was apparently posted on the right, and probably Buchannan's as well, while Holburne's and Gray's regiments were on the left . Where Barclay's men were posted is unclear. They too may have been on the left, but Lambert says that a 'pass', in front of Holburne's right, was "lined by the enemy's musketeers", and this is perhaps a more likely location.

From subsequent events it would appear that Sir John Browne's cavalry brigade was on the right, and that an ad hoc one comprising Brechin's

*Scots musketeer - one of a number of mercenaries seen in Stettin in the 1630s.*

Horse and Augustine's 'Mossers' was on the left.

As for the English:

We were more in number, in my judgement, by at least five or six hundred, but on the other side the enemy had the advantage of the ground, our left wing of horse being upon a very ill ground, where was a pass lined by the enemy's musketeers;

Upon consideration whereof, we placed our greatest strength in our right wing, consisting of my own regiment of horse, and two of colonel Lidcot's, and two of colonel Okey's troops; the charge of that wing being left with him; and in the left only four troops of colonel Okey's and two of Lidcot's, to whom the charge of that wing was committed.

The battle [centre] consisting of mine and colonel Daniel's regiment of foot, and reserved by colonel west and colonel Syler's regiment, being commanded by colonel Overton.

*The original part of Pitreavie Castle.*

*Maclean monument, a short distance from Pitreavie Castle and near the crossed swords on the ordnance survey map.*

Both sides were now deployed in order of battle, but nothing happened for another hour and a half. Lambert tells us he was still expecting the Scots to attack him 'being come so far to seek us', while Holburne, having been prevented from retreating, was similarly expecting to be attacked.

At length the stalemate was broken when Lambert received word from Cromwell that reinforcements were marching from Stirling to Holburne's assistance and that as he himself was pulling back to Linlithgow it was likely that even more would be sent shortly. Rather disappointingly Lambert, having described his initial movements and deployment in some detail, then rather blandly states that it was therefore 'resolved we should climb the hill to them, which accordingly we did, and through the Lord's strength, put them to an absolute rout'.

There was of course a little more to it than that. Browne, leading the Scots cavalry on the right (or western side of the battlefield), charged forward and with the advantages of the slope and their lances, broke some of the English cavalry opposite. These were presumably Lytcott's raw troopers, but Browne may have had to put in everything he had to achieve this, and had no reserves to exploit his initial success. Certainly the upshot was that Lytcott counter-attacked with his own reserves and routed the lot, capturing Browne in the process. Similarly, on the left (Inverkeithing side) Augustine and Brechin were initially successful, but the Moss Troopers were pretty undisciplined and Brechin's men scarcely less so. Once again they were completely routed by Okey's reserve – probably led in by Lambert himself, who collected two pistol balls lodged between his armour and his coat.

With the Scots cavalry well scattered, it was the turn of the infantry. There is no real evidence of a serious fight at this stage of the battle. Indeed Lambert states that it was all over in a very short time. This, taken with a curious statement in the *Fraser Chronicles* that 'Hellish Hoburn came not up, which if he had the Scotch had carried it but doubt', suggests that the Scots cavalry either charged to cover the retreat of the infantry, or, more likely, that Holburne, seeing all was going to pot, simply made off leaving them to their fate.

Either way, just as at Dunbar, their retreat must have been prolonged and nightmarish experience. Holburne's own veterans and Gray's regiment both seem to have escaped more or less intact, although an oral tradition relates that the

*Although McIan used this heroic figure battling Cromwellian troopers to illustrate the Mac Millan tartan, he undoubtedly had the last stand of Duart's clansmen at Pitreavie in mind.*

MAC MILLAN

Pinkerton Burn ran with blood for three days afterwards. Both Buchannan's and Duart's regiments on the other hand, fleeing across the open valley to the west of the burn were effectively destroyed after a four hour running battle. Afterwards Lambert, claiming to have taken 1,400 prisoners including Browne and Buchannan, commented that more were killed than taken because 'divers of them were Highlanders, and had very ill quarter; and indeed I am persuaded few of them escaped without a knock'. Be that as it may, however the numbers might be computed, their long retreat ended on the hill-slopes around Pitreavie Castle, some two kilometres due north of their original position on Castland Hill.

Tradition relates that the Highlanders sought refuge in the castle, but the owners, a family named Wardlaw, not only refused them admittance but actually threw stones down on them from the roof. With Lambert's men closing in fast, Duart and his men turned at bay. He himself was killed, but not before seven of his clansmen had interposed themselves one by one, crying *Fear eile airson Eachainn!* ( 'Another for Hector!'). Legend has it that all but thirty-five out of 800 [sic] of the Highlanders were killed, though, more realistically, Sir James Balfour records that the Scots lost about 800 men in *total*, of whom no more than 100 were Duart's clansmen.

It was by any reckoning a quick and decisive victory won by Lambert at the cost of 'not above eight men, but divers wounded'. More importantly it secured the bridgehead and, over the next two days, Cromwell shipped over another four regiments, and then followed himself with virtually his whole army. By 26 July he reported that he had 13-14,000 men across and on 31 July he marched on Perth which surrendered to him on 2 August. Shy of fighting in the open ever since Dunbar, Leslie had made no attempt to engage him, and now with his lines of communication very firmly cut, he fell in with the King's desperate notion of marching into England in a vain attempt to rally the English Royalists for one last throw of the dice. With the army gone, and soon to be destroyed at Worcester, Scotland was all but powerless to resist the last English invasion. Stirling Castle surrendered on 15 August 1651, Dundee was stormed and sacked on 1 September and Aberdeen was occupied without a fight a week later. The last of the field armies, commanded by the Marquis of Huntly and the Earl of Balcarres had surrendered by 3 December, and, with the surrender of Dunottar Castle on 24 May 1652, it was all over.

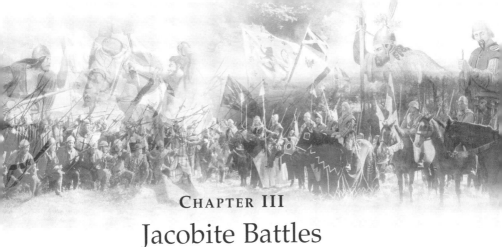

## CHAPTER III

# Jacobite Battles

✠

## *Warriors: Redcoats and Clansmen*

The battles described so far were largely fought between armies which, broadly speaking, were trained and equipped in a similar manner. The armies differed only in so far as one side or the other may have employed a larger proportion of archers or spearmen or cavalry on the day of the fight. The three battles described in this final part of the triptych, however, saw very markedly different armies pitted against each other.

In 1707 the Scots and English armies were combined to become the British Army whose organisation, equipment and tactical doctrines had evolved in a steady but quite recognisable fashion from those employed in the civil wars.

The pike, obsolete at last, had been entirely replaced by the musket or firelock, which was now fired by means of what is generally known as the flintlock. The clamp holding a length of burning slow-match was replaced by a smaller and more elegant spring loaded one that struck a piece of flint against a steel in order to create a shower of sparks with which to ignite the priming charge in the flash-pan. Otherwise it was little changed and although the powder flasks had been replaced by individual paper cartridges the loading process remained similar enough to require the same generous allowance of space for each man standing in the ranks.

The tendency towards more linear formations noted in the previous section grew more marked with the advent of the eighteenth century. Infantry battalions now drew up in only three ranks, which, with a little jostling and pushing, dignified by the term 'locking', sufficed to let every man fire at once should the requirement arise. In point of fact however the old system of firing by ranks had for the moment been given over in favour of a tactic known as platooning.

There were a number of variants, but essentially platooning required the men to be told off into platoons of twenty-thirty men apiece which were then designated as one of three 'firings'. At the commencement of the action only those belonging to the first firing would discharge their weapons either in a ripple from one end of the line to the other, or else inward to the centre from the flanks. Having begun they would then be followed in quick succession by the platoons of the second and third firings. Just as in the days of blazing away by ranks it was hopefully assumed that the platoons of the first firing would have reloaded by the time those belonging to the third had discharged.

Platooning was once again designed to maintain a steady rolling fire over a prolonged period of time, but as was about to become uncomfortably apparent it was ill-adapted to stop a determined assault by an enemy who insisted on charging forward rather than obligingly halting to return fire. Bluntly put, with no more than a third of the battalion delivering a sputtering fire at any one time, it was all but impossible to kill enough of the attackers quickly enough to stop them.

Frequently, those attackers were Highland clansmen.

There had of course been Highlanders in the ranks of one or other of the armies engaged in all of the battles previously described, but with the single exception of Kilsyth the clansmen had invariably been in a minority and were often no differently trained and equipped than anyone else. Indeed it would be fair to say that unless mustered with other pikemen in the ranks of the schiltrons, Highlanders were widely regarded as unreliable levies who might make useful scouts but otherwise served only to make up the numbers.

That perception was about to change dramatically. During the civil wars the Royalist Marquis of Montrose's army had largely been comprised of levies from the north-east of Scotland, stiffened by Irish mercenaries, both of whom were conventionally equipped with pikes and muskets. From time to time however he was also joined by Highland contingents and at Kilsyth they actually accounted for more than half his infantry. This did not materially affect either the conduct or the outcome of the battle, but in its immediate aftermath their ruthless slaughter of Baillie's Fife levies earned them a new and terrifying reputation as bloodthirsty savages - a perception which was reinforced by the massacre of General Mackay's army at Killiecrankie in 1689.

The success of the fearsome Highland charge in fact depended very much upon this, rather than physically hacking through the enemy formation with their swords. Lieutenant General Henry Hawley, who served against the Jacobite clans at Sherriffmuir in 1715, stressed this point in instructions issued to his troops before meeting them for a second time at Falkirk in 1746:

> They Commonly form their Front rank of what they call their best men, or True Highlanders, the number of which being allways but few, when they form in Battallions they commonly form four deep, & these Highlanders form the front of the four, the rest being lowlanders & arrant scum. When these battalions come within a large musket shott or three score yards [50 metres] this front rank gives their fire, and immediately throw down their firelocks and come down in a cluster with their swords and targets, making a noise and endeavouring to pierce the body or battalion before them – becoming twelve or fourteen deep by the time they come up to the people they attack.

Hawley then went on to describe his patent method to 'demolish' them – which will be described in its proper place – but it is perhaps worth emphasising the point that it was only the 'true highlanders' in the front rank who were armed with broadsword and targe, and that those who followed behind were a much less well equipped rabble who served only to intimidate, and, if successful, to slaughter the fugitives. Essentially the whole process boiled down to the simple question of whether or not the attacking clansmen could scare their opponents into running away, for if they did not the charge would all too often come to a faltering halt well short of its objective.

## *Sheriffmuir*

Restored to the throne in 1660, Charles II was succeeded in 1685 by his younger brother James, who was an able administrator and competent professional soldier. Arguably he was far too able. He was also a Roman Catholic, which might not have mattered too much had he been forced to rely upon his parliaments to run his kingdoms, but he soon began shaping up as an effective absolute ruler, in the model of his fellow Catholic, the Sun King, Louis XIV. Of itself this was disquieting enough, but when he produced a Catholic son and heir in 1688, some of the English magnates invited his son-in-law, Prince William of Orange, to challenge him for the throne. William responded with alacrity and landed his forces at Torbay in Devon, while James, suffering from a quite uncharacteristic failure of nerve, fled to France. The English parliament hurriedly accepted this flight as a de facto abdication and proclaimed a Glorious Revolution, but north of the border events took a grimmer turn.

Cleaving to the ancient principle that the King reigned only by the will of his people, the Estates stoutly declared that he had forfaultit the croun and offered it instead to William. However there was still substantial support for James, particularly in the Highlands, and one of his officers, John Graham of Claverhouse raised the first of the Jacobite armies, only to be killed in the moment of victory at Killiecrankie in 1689. It took another three years for the rising to run its course and culminate in the Glencoe business, but it is worth emphasising that all but one of the redcoated units overrun at Killiecrankie was Scottish. Neither this nor any of the succeeding Jacobite Risings would be a straightforward contest between the Scots and the English, indeed in 1707 at the height of a major war with France, their two countries were formally joined and thereafter the rules changed.

The Union was deeply unpopular at just about every level in Scottish society and the Jacobites now sought to capitalise on that unpopularity by assuming leadership of the campaign to dissolve it. In the short term this strategy was extremely effective, but nevertheless the Stuarts' eyes remained fixed on Whitehall and the contradictions inherent in pursuing a claim to the throne of England with armies largely made up of men dedicated to severing all links with that country became tragically apparent in both 1715 and 1745.

There had already been an abortive uprising in 1708 when young James arrived in the Firth of Forth with a French fleet, but before he could land the Royal Navy appeared on the scene. Thereupon for reasons which are still unclear the French admiral incontinent fled, and the rising was stillborn. In retrospect this was the Jacobites' last best chance, for the war ended in 1713 and the immediate prospect of further French assistance evaporated. In the meantime Dutch William had died in 1702, to be succeeded by Anne, the last of James VII's daughters and she in turn died on 1 August leaving no direct heir. Instead there were two candidates for the throne. The obvious one was of course her half-brother James, but the successful one turned out to be another great grandson of James VI – George, Elector of Hanover.

Nevertheless George was a far from a popular choice. He enjoyed considerable support in the army since he had served under the great Duke of Marlborough during the late war. He was a Protestant and therefore politically more acceptable than his Catholic cousin. Unfortunately he was also a foreigner who could not even speak English. Worse still he had no sense of the political currents operating in his new-found kingdom and proceeded to alienate a number of influential figures from the very moment he stepped ashore.

One of them was John Erskine, Earl of Mar. He was a politician of some ability who had been Secretary of State for Scotland under Queen Anne, but George decided to make a clean sweep of the Queen's men and bring in his own supporters. No matter that Mar presented him with the customary loyal address, the King's only response was to demand that he surrender his seals of office. Unsurprisingly Mar responded in his turn by casting his lot with the Jacobites and formally raised King James's standard at Braemar in Aberdeenshire on 6 September 1715.

Large numbers of recruits soon came flooding in from the north-east and by 28 September he and his rapidly growing army were at Perth, but there they stopped to await reinforcements and, arguably, lost the initiative forever. The Government had already responded to reports of the uprising by sending Major General Joseph Wightman and three regiments of infantry to Stirling at the end of August in order to secure both the castle and the

## PRINCES AND PRETENDERS

*The various designations applied to the Jacobite leaders can be rather confusing, since in the first place the later Stuarts bore two orders of precedence. When King James succeeded Elizabeth I as King of England in 1603, he was still styled James VI when in Scotland, but James I when in his new kingdom of England. Similarly his grandson, was styled James VII in Scotland and James II in England. Although never crowned, his great grandson also assumed the styles of James VIII and James III.*

*The latter was also referred to by his opponents as the 'Pretender' (to the throne) and then, after the advent of his son, Prince Charles Edward Stuart, as the 'Old Pretender' by way of distinguishing him from Charles, who thus became the 'Young Pretender'.*

*In the meantime, James had served with the French Army at the battle of Ramillies under the transparent pseudonym of the Chevalier St. George. Thereafter he was discreetly referred to by his friends as 'The Chevalier', and, in time, as 'The Old Chevalier' to distinguish him from his son 'The Young Chevalier'.*

*Finally it is worth noting that the Young Chevalier's other nickname, 'Bonnie Prince Charlie', derives from the Gaelic version of Charles - Tearlach.*

vital Forth crossings. Sensibly enough all three regiments were Scottish; the Earl of Orrery's was better known as the Scots Fusiliers, while Shannon's was the Edinburgh Regiment, now the King's Own Scottish Borderers, and the third was the Buffs, which although nominally English had a Scottish colonel (the Earl of Forfar), Scottish officers and a considerable number of Scots soldiers in the ranks at this time.

Shortly afterwards the three infantry units were joined at Stirling by the two regiments of cavalry customarily stationed in Scotland for policing duties – one of them Portmore's Royal (Scots) Dragoons – but their numbers were still perilously low. At the end of Queen Anne's war the three infantry regiments had been reduced to cadre strength and now could only muster some 320 rank and file apiece, while the two dragoon regiments each had only about 180 troopers.

Consequently two additional cavalry regiments were ordered up from England and more reinforcements promised. At the same time the Duke of Argyle – Red John of the Battles – was appointed Commander in Chief Scotland, but when he arrived in the camp at Stirling on 16 September he found that he still had only about 1,840

*The 'Old Pretender' the titular King James VIII of Scotland and II of England.*

men to face Mar's estimated 6,000. Three little battalions of loyalist volunteers, numbering 600 in all, turned up from Glasgow over the next few days, but if Mar had continued his advance from Perth at the end of the month or even in early October there would have been very little Argyle could have done to stop him.

Mar's problem was that he was out of his depth – and he knew it. He was a career politician, not a soldier. He had successfully raised an army for King James and, with very little effort, found himself in effective control of most of Scotland north of the Forth, but thus far neither James, nor his soldier half-brother the Duke of Berwick, had appeared on the scene. Conscious of his military limitations, Mar expected to hand the army over to his master on his arrival and so the last thing he wanted to do in the meantime was to lose it, or significantly damage it in a battle that he knew himself unqualified to manage.

Thus both sides waited. Argyle at Stirling for reinforcements, and Mar at Perth for the King. The difference was that Argyle could afford to wait, Mar could not.

Nevertheless the Jacobites, or 'Jacks' as they were more familiarly known, were not entirely inactive. In early October they moved into Fife and from there nearly half the army, led by MacIntosh of Borlum, embarked on fishing boats and crossed the Forth under cover of darkness to launch an abortive attack on Edinburgh on 14 October. They seem to have had some hopes of the city going over to them, but in the event the gates remained firmly shut and they had to settle for seizing Leith.

This provoked a considerable flurry of activity. Argyle immediately rushed down from Stirling with 100 dragoons and 200 mounted infantry and threw

*A fine study of a Highland clansman in belted plaid by McIan.*

MAC GILLIVRAY

*Braemar Castle – where the rebel standard was raised.*

himself into Edinburgh that night. Next morning, backed up by a somewhat motley array including the Edinburgh Town Guard, the loyalist Edinburgh Volunteers, and at least three militia regiments, he and his regulars marched down to Leith and demanded the rebels' surrender. Naturally enough the 'Jacks', who had ensconced themselves in the old citadel, treated this demand with the contempt it deserved. Although the citadel, last repaired by Cromwell's men in the 1650s, was in a very dilapidated state it still presented a formidable obstacle to an attacker unprovided with artillery – which at this point was the one thing Argyle lacked.

So he drew off again, despite Sir John Clerk of Penicuik's complaint that 'we who knew the citadel never doubted but dismounted Dragoons cou'd force the place sword in hand'. Instead, Argyle planned to bring some heavy guns and mortars down from the Castle, in order to batter the rebels into submission rather than waste his precious regulars in a vainglorious assault for the entertainment of the militia. However that night, Borlum took the opportunity to get out again while the going was good. The citadel was supposedly still being watched by the loyalists, including two regiments of militia from the Merse and Teviotdale, but at low tide the rebels marched away over the sands to Seton House, near the future battlefield of Prestonpans.

Argyle prepared to go after them, but on the same day Mar tentatively moved forward to Auchterarder and on 17 October headed for Dunblane. Warned in time, Argyle dashed back, leaving Edinburgh at noon and arriving in Stirling at about 8.00pm. Disappointed, Mar returned to Perth next day, and the day after that Borlum and his men marched south to a rendezvous at Kelso with another group of rebels from the Borders and Northumberland. They would eventually march into England, to fight and then surrender at Preston, but so far as Mar was concerned they were out of the equation.

Argyle can scarcely have been happy at the notion of Borlum's men and other groups of insurgents floating around in his rear, but he was still determined to hold the vital Forth crossings and as the days wore on he at last began to receive badly needed reinforcements. Mar too was joined by more than enough men to replace those sent off with Borlum, including the western clans who came in on 5 November, and eventually even he recognised that he could delay marching no longer.

On 10 November 1715 the Jacobite army marched south from Perth, intending to force their way across the Forth just a short distance above Stirling. No fewer than three diversionary attacks were planned in order to distract attention from the main crossing point, but it seemingly never occurred to anyone that instead of obligingly waiting to be imposed upon, Argyle might come out to meet them head on.

Consequently the Jacobite advance displayed very little sense of urgency. Having marched as far as Auchterarder on the first day, Mar decided to halt there and await the return of two battalions under Lord George Murray and Stewart of Invernytie which had earlier been sent into Fife on a tax gathering sweep. In the meantime he spent the day in reviewing his army on Auchterarder Moor. This seems to have been necessary to sort out the exact order of battle and even some aspects of the command structure, for, according to the Master of Sinclair, the cavalry in particular argued 'about the posts of our squadrons, and were never so constant in anything as our being disorderlie'. Next day, with no sign of either Murray or Invernytie, the advance resumed along the right side of Allan Water towards the little village of Kinbuck. The rebel advance guard, presumably tasked with carrying out the diversionary attacks, was to have carried on as far as Dunblane, but instead they began to receive disquieting reports that Argyle was already there.

Initially Mar was sceptical, but by nightfall the reports had been confirmed

*Highland clansman with turcael – a basket hilted sword with a curved 'Turkish' blade. Based on one of a remarkable series of sketches by an artist from Penicuik in 1745.*

Jacobites advance uphill in two columns towards camera

Kinbuch Muir

*The north side of Sheriffmuir as viewed from the crest. The initial Jacobite position was on Kinbuck Muir, directly in the centre at middle distance. The rebel army marched directly up this slope to form its battle-line just behind camera.*

and having closed up to Kinbuck the whole army halted there. The weather was very cold with a hard frost and as the ever-acerbic Sinclair grumbled, never were so many men 'packt up so close together since the invention of pouder'.

At 6.00am the next morning, Sunday, 13 November, the 'Jacks' stiffly moved out of the village and long before dawn formed up in order of battle on some high ground to the east, presumably Kinbuck Muir. Their initial deployment was straightforward enough: two lines of infantry, with the cavalry posted on either wing.

From left to right the front line, commanded by Lieutenant General Alexander Gordon of Auchintoul, comprised all the recently arrived western clans: Stewart of Appin's Regiment (260); Cameron of Locheil's (300); MacDonald of Glencoe's (150); Sir John MacLean's (350); Allan MacDonald of Clanranald's (565); two battalions raised by the Earl of Breadalbane but actually commanded by Campbell of Glenlyon (400); Alexander MacDonnell of Glengarry's Regiment (460) which included the Grants of Glen Urquhart and Glenmoriston; and Sir Donald MacDonald of Sleat's Regiment (700).

If correct the figures quoted for each unit would produce a total of some 3,185 infantry in the front line, although this is probably more than a little optimistic. The second line – effectively Mar's original army – under Major General George Hamilton, was not quite so strong, comprising; a battalion of Athollmen under Struan Robertson (200); Lord Panmure's Regiment (420); a battalion of Lord Drummond's Regiment, commanded by Lord Strathallan (250); two battalions of the Marquis of Huntly's regiment, led by Ogilvy of Boyne and Gordon of

*The ridge where the Jacobites formed their battle-line as seen from Argyle's position down by what is now Sheriffmuir Road. There is no mention of any trees on the moor in 1715.*

Glenbuchat respectively (400); and two more battalions under the Earl of Seaforth (400); totalling a further 1,670 men.

Mar also had a number of cavalry, under the overall command of Lieutenant General Lord Drummond. They varied considerably in quality. Some, perhaps most, were mounted on proper riding horses, but about half of Huntly's men were Highlanders mounted on garrons, so small that the 'light horsemen' (as he termed them to everyone's amusement) trailed their feet on the ground. The right wing, commanded by the Earl Marischal, was intended to comprise the Marischal's own regiment (180); a small troop of Stirlingshire gentlemen under Lord Kilsyth (seventy-seven) and Huntly's two squadrons (400). The left, under the command of the Master of Sinclair, was to have been made up of just three small units raised in Perthshire (seventy); Fife (ninety) and Forfarshire (100).

In the event nothing, let alone the dispositions, went according to plan. Despite the bitter cold, Argyle had spent the night in the open just to the east, or more likely south east of Dunblane, and shortly before first light he set out with a reconnaissance party to look for the 'Jacks'.

Just who saw whom first is probably immaterial. The sun came up at around 8.00am and at about that point the rebels noticed 'a command of horse on the high ground to the south of us'. This was of course Argyle and his escort, but at least a couple of hours seem to have passed before the Earl Marischal was sent up on to

*This painting by McIan provides an excellent illustration of one of Huntly's 'Light Horse'.*

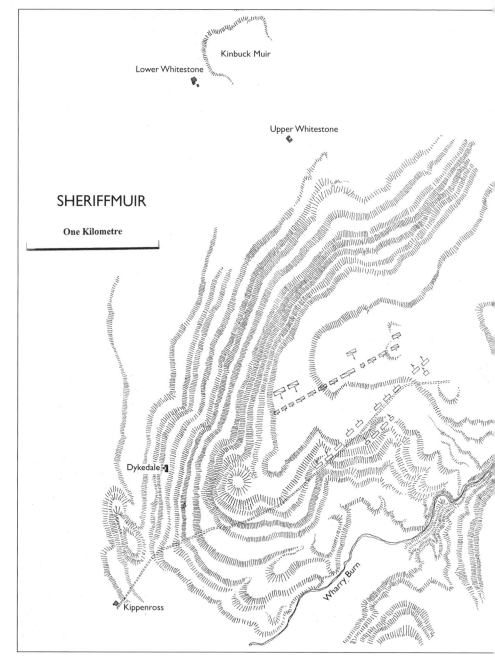

## SHERIFFMUIR

**One Kilometre**

Kinbuck Muir

Lower Whitestone

Upper Whitestone

Dykedale

Kippenross

Wharry Burn

*Presumed initial dispositions. On the night before the battle the Jacobites were stuffed into Kinbuck and in the early morning formed up in two lines on Kinbuck Muir between Balhaldie and Lower Whitestone. Argyle's men were encamped somewhere to the south-east of Dunblane. The lone Jacobite cavalry unit positioned behind the left centre of the line is the Earl Marischal's squadron, standing beside the gathering stone.*

the Sheriffmuir with his own squadron and Sleat's Highlanders to drive him off. Having seen all he needed to see, Argyle prudently retired. No doubt he regretted that he had not called his own army forward in the meantime. It had been recognised on both sides that the battle was going to have to be fought on the top of the moor and that whoever established himself on the crest first was obviously going to enjoy a significant advantage.

For the moment the Jacobites held the initiative for although the movements of Sleat's men are a little unclear, the Marischal's squadron, commanded by his brother James Keith (the future Prussian Feld Marschal) remained up on the ridge, close by the so-called gathering stone. Then at about 11.30am the Earl of Mar started leading up the rest of his army:

> which he did [recalled Keith] in too much haste; for the army, which marched in four columns, arrived in such confusion that it was impossible to form them according to the line of battle projected, every one posted himself as he found ground, and one column of foot enclining to the right and another to the left of the Earl Marischal's squadron of horse, that regiment which should have been on the tight, found itself in the centre, separated from the rest of the horse and opposed to the enemies foot; our foot formed all in one line, except on the left, where a bog hinder'd them from extending themselves, and encreased the confusion.

If anything Keith may have understated the degree of confusion in the Jacobite ranks. What seems to have happened is that the two lines of infantry turned to their left into columns of march and headed diagonally up the hill, being followed by the two wings of cavalry, and somewhere in the rear by five cannon. For regular troops this was a fairly straightforward manoeuvre and indeed the normal way of deploying for battle. Once in position they should simply have faced to their front to again stand in their two lines. Instead, whether by accident or design, through a panicky decision to throw as many men as possible on to the crest, or just through sheer ineptitude, the infantry formed up in just one line on either side of the Marischal's squadron, on a frontage of about 1800 metres. Keith's account clearly shows that the western clans were on the right, and that the various regiments making up the original second line now formed the left wing. Whether the individual regiments formed up in the same order as before may also be doubted for Keith implies that each one deployed as it came up. This would probably have made no difference to the western clans – although there is some evidence that all the MacDonalds now stood together – but it almost certainly meant that the order of the former second line units was reversed with Struan Robertson's men coming to a halt by the Marischal's squadron and Huntly's and Seaforth's regiments ending up on the far left instead of the right.

A further complication was that the ground on the left – to the east of the gathering stone – turned out to be too boggy for the troops to deploy properly. The extent of the problem is unclear, but it seems likely that Huntly's men formed the furtherest extremity of this wing and that Seaforth's men were stuffed behind them. The boggy ground in this area probably also accounts for the otherwise

*The MacRae memorial commemorating the nearby sacrifice of the Earl of Seaforth's men. Marked on the Ordnance Survey map this is an excellent starting point for a tour of the battlefield.*

inexplicable massing of all the Jacobite cavalry, (except the Marischal's squadron of course) on the right wing. It was certainly not by accident, for the Master of Sinclair declared that the order came by way of three separate messengers: 'Ane Aide-de-Camp of Kilseyth... someone from Mar, and one Lewis Innes from my lord Huntlie, by Mar's order'. This last may be significant for Huntly at least must have been aware of the bog. Whatever the reason, it was probably just as well that all the horse were drawn together for Sinclair's 260 amateurs can scarcely have been expected to stand up to the 360 veteran troopers of Portmore's and Evans' Dragoons who would have faced them on the left wing.

A little further to the south, Argyle was carrying out exactly the same manoeuvre, but if anything with even less success. It has been suggested that his men spent the night around Dykedale but the slope of the ridge is rather steep there and it is far too close to the eventual battlefield. It is much more likely that they were actually on the more level ground further to the south by Kippenross. He too ordered his men to face to the flank and ascend the hill in column of march presumably along the trackway now known as Sheriffmuir Road. Leading the advance, and therefore destined to form the extreme right of his line when it halted and faced north, were Portmore's Dragoons (180) and Evans' Dragoons (180), backed up by about sixty loyalist volunteer horse led by the Earl of Rothes. Then came Lord Forfar's Foot (320); Wightman's (250); Shannon's (340); Morrison's (240); Montagu's (240) and Clayton's Foot (240). The left wing comprised Kerr's Dragoons (180) and Carpenter's Dragoons (180). The second line, or rather the reserve was made up of just two battalions; Egerton's (250) and Orrery's Scots Fusiliers (320), flanked by the two squadrons of Stair's Dragoons (180).

Yet something went seriously wrong, for Argyle's men had a far shorter distance to cover and there is no obvious reason why they should not have been able to get up on to the high ground long before the Jacobites. For some reason the regulars must have taken a very long time to get underway, because not only did the rebels win the race, but some of Argyle's regiments were still struggling to get into position when they arrived, as Keith noted with satisfaction:

> The Duke of Argyle was no less embarrassed on his side. His army was not yet entirely formed; the rear, which was to have formed his left wing, was yet on their march, and showed us their flanck, which being observed by Lieutenant General Gordon, he order'd our troops immerdiately to charge, which they did with so much vigour that in less than ten minutes they entirely defeated six regiments of foot and five squadrons of dragoons, which composed more than half of the Duke's army.

But the attack almost faltered at the very outset, when MacDonald of Clanranald was shot off his horse and killed, although Glengarry (whose regiment may now have been adjacent) immediately rushed forward shouting 'Revenge! Revenge! Today for revenge and tomorrow for mourning!'. This was enough. The Highlanders rushed forward sword in hand, the disorganised regulars melted away in front of them, and the whole lot; clansmen, redcoats, dragoons and rebel cavalry tumbled straight down the hillside into the valley of the Wharry Burn, where something of a massacre took place. Only General Whetham, with Carpenter's Dragoons, escaped the rout and after a half-hearted counter attack drew off to the flank in tolerable good order. Some of the fugitives however ran all the way back to Stirling, where they unsurprisingly reported a total defeat.

Argyle's official report chronicles the fate of those who did not escape. Morrison's Regiment lost Lieutenant Colonel Hanmers, two captains, four lieutenants, three ensigns missing 'and a considerable number of privates'. Montagu's Regiment had Lieutenant Colonel Laurence, Captain Umball and Captain Bernard missing, 'and a considerable number of privates killed'. Clayton's Regiment suffered Captain Barlow killed, whilst the Scots Fusiliers lost Captain

Cheissly, Lieutenant Hayard and Lieutenant Michelson missing (said to be taken), Captain Urquhart of Burdsyards badly wounded and taken prisoner. Egerton's Regiment had Captain Danaer wounded, 'and a few privates killed'.

Although not entirely satisfactory in that the information is obviously incomplete, this dismal catalogue is nevertheless quite informative in showing that the weight of the rebel attack actually fell on what was effectively Argyle's centre; that is Morrisons and Montagu's regiments in the front line and the Scots Fusiliers behind them. On the other hand, Clayton's, on the extreme left of the line were quite literally brushed aside and although certainly routed may have got away with comparatively few casualties. Similarly, Egerton's, on the right of the second line may have been shielded to some extent by Shannon's Edinburgh Regiment, which would account for their losing only one captain wounded and those 'few privates killed'.

With the obvious exception of Clanranald, it is unlikely that there were many casualties amongst the victorious western clans, but they were certainly well scattered and totally disorganised. Some may well have left the battlefield altogether while others fell to stripping and robbing the dead and wounded. Consequently it took nearly four hours for Mar and Gordon to reassemble a respectable body of men, particularly since all of them 'were extremely fatigued and had eat nothing in two days'. Eventually they marched them back up again to where Sinclair and his three little squadrons were still standing on a prominent knoll known as the 'Stoney Hill of Kippendavie', about 1,300 metres south west of the gathering stone. There they learned that the battle was far from over.

The Jacobite left wing, commanded by Hamilton, had gone forward at about the same time as the right, only to meet with disaster. In the first place Shannon's, Wightman's and Forfar's regiments were properly formed up and much readier to face the onslaught than their unfortunate comrades further down the hill. Secondly, since that the rebels attacking them were largely Lowlanders, it is likely that the attack on this wing was much less ferocious than the one launched by the western clans – which, given that the rebel tactics depended on intimidation rather than brute force, may have been significant. What decided the affair however was Argyle's two regiments of dragoons on this wing; Portmore's Scots Greys, commanded by Lord Cathcart, and Evans' Dragoons.

*Another clansman, or perhaps even a lowland Jacobite, after the Penicuik artist. Hundreds of these so-called 'Lochaber' axes were supplied by the burgh of Aberdeen to equip the Jacobite army in 1715.*

At first the fighting was inconclusive, which is probably a polite way of saying that instead of obligingly running away the regulars stood their ground, while the rebels halted some distance away and both exchanged an ineffectual fire. There may however have been some isolated contacts along the line for the British army's casualties included the Earl of Forfar, who was particularly described as having been 'shot in the knee, and cut in the head with ten or twelve strokes from their broad swords, after quarter'. In other words he was brought down by a shot in the knee and then more or less hacked to death while he lay or sat on the ground.

In contrast to what was then going on down in the Wharry Burn however, the other casualties were very light; an ensign and just eight men of Forfar's reported as killed, two or three men killed in Wightmans and five or six men killed and wounded in Shannon's. Nearly all of them presumably were gunshot wounds.

With the assault stalled, Argyle ordered his cavalry to move around to their right and come in on the rebels' open flank, which they did with considerable success. Hamilton's left was certainly broken and the MacRae monument commemorates the complete destruction of two of Seaforth's companies from Kintail. The rest of Hamilton's regiments fell back down the hill as well, but although a fair number of prisoners were taken, including Lord Strathallan, the dragoons were unable to pursue them with the proper vigour because of the marshy ground. According to Sinclair the frost had frozen the surface into a crust that could support the weight of a man but not a horse. At any rate although some of the Jacobites fled all the way back to Allan Water and beyond – the Marquis of Huntly was particularly criticised for the speed of his departure – Hamilton managed to rally a number of regiments, only for the dragoons to attack again. In fact one account claims that they attacked no fewer than twelve times before Hamilton was eventually driven from the field. It is hard to see how, but it is rather more likely that Hamilton, acutely aware that the rest of the army had completely disappeared and perhaps not entirely convinced that the battle was won, conducted a reasonably orderly withdrawal to Allan Water, harassed by the dragoons. With the ground treacherous underfoot they for their part were probably content to simply hustle them along rather than try anything more dramatic. Like their infantry colleagues they too suffered only a handful of casualties, but it may be significant that they included both Major General Evans, and his lieutenant colonel, a certain Henry Hawley.

In the meantime Argyle had rather belatedly realised that half of his own army had been swept away, and hurriedly began reorganising those who were left. He formed a battle-line somewhere on the north slope of the Sheriffmuir with his remaining infantry in the centre, Portmore's Dragoons (and perhaps Rothes' volunteers) on the right and Evans' Dragoons and the remaining squadron of Stair's on the left. A single cannon was placed in front of the cavalry on either wing and the whole lot took up a reasonably strong position facing south (ie. back the way they had come) among 'some Enclosures and mud Walls, which would serve for a Breast-Work in Case they were attack'd'. The exact location of this position is uncertain, but oddly enough Keith, who was watching with a keen eye, claimed that it was the same place the Jacobites had spent the previous night. While the description certainly does not fit the village of Kinbuck, it may however point to one of the farms on Kinbuck Muir, probably Upper Whitestone.

Whatever the actual location of Argyle's little band, there was to be no more fighting there that day, for by now it was about 4.00pm and nightfall was at hand. Some of the Jacobite leaders reckoned there was time enough for one last attack to finish the business, but nothing happened and eventually Argyle retired to Dunblane under cover of darkness. Mar hovered about ineffectually for another day, then retired to Perth and thereafter the collapse of the rebellion was only a matter of time.

James eventually landed at Peterhead on 22 December, but exhausted by the midwinter voyage, did not arrive in Perth until 9 January. Three weeks later at a council of war Mar announced that the intention was 'not to Retreat only, but to put an end to the Design in general for a time'. And so it was. James returned to France with Mar as quietly as he had come, and General Gordon disbanded what remained of the army at Ruthven in Badenoch on 14 February 1716.

# Prestonpans

By 1745 the Stuarts' increasingly shaky claim to the British crown was all but moribund, and assessments by Jacobite agents gloomily warned that if another rising was not launched very soon any remaining support for the Stuarts would be lost by default. Even more worryingly, most of those who were still prepared to commit themselves to the cause bluntly stated that outside assistance was essential and that they would rise in the event of a French landing, but not otherwise.

It was unfortunate that France initially displayed very little interest in an invasion, for her principal priorities lay with continental Europe. Nevertheless, in 1744, a substantial force was put together in readiness for a descent in the Thames Estuary, and another, albeit smaller force, was earmarked for Scotland. However, the primary object of this expedition was not to be the restoration of the Stuarts, but the neutralising of British intervention in the War of the Austrian Succession which was then raging in Germany. Consequently when Channel storms unexpectedly disrupted the embarkation and scattered the French battle-fleet, the expedition was abandoned with few obvious signs of regret and the would-be invaders were marched into Flanders instead.

Behind them they left Prince Charles Edward Stuart, the elder son and heir of the would-be king, James. With his father's commission as Prince Regent in his pocket, he had made a dramatic journey northwards from Italy in order to go ashore with the invasion force, but instead he was left impotently kicking his heels in Paris. Then in the summer of 1745 he was offered help from a most unlikely

*McIan painting based on a portrait of the Duke of Perth, one of the Jacobite leaders at Prestonpans.*

source – the substantial colony of Irish Jacobite exiles in Brittany. Many of them, naturally enough, were ship-owners and Lord Clare, the commander of the French Army's famed Irish Brigade, introduced one particular consortium to the Prince. Headed by Walter Routledge and Anthony Walsh, this company had originally been engaged in the slave trade between Africa and the West Indies, but, as traffic was seriously disrupted by the war, they turned to privateering instead. Now, for an unspecified price, they were prepared to carry the Prince and his supporters to Scotland.

On 5 July 1745 the consortium's two ships cleared Belle Isle and after fighting off a British frigate, HMS *Lion,* the Prince was safely landed on the Hebriddean island of Eriskay on 23 July. There he met with an unexpectedly unfriendly welcome. Far from bringing a French army he had just seven companions and hardly any money or equipment. Not surprisingly the locals flatly refused to join him and instead he was rather brusquely advised to turn around and go home again. Retorting that he had come home, he instead moved on to the mainland and entered into a desperate round of negotiations with other potential supporters. Some measure of his difficulty in persuading them to commit themselves is the fact that the rebel standard was not raised until nearly a month later, at Glenfinnan on 19 August. By that time the Government was only too well aware of what was going on and the Commander-in-Chief Scotland had been ordered into the Highlands.

The forces available to Lieutenant General Sir John Cope were far from prepossessing either in numbers or in quality. Even on paper he could muster little more than three battalions of infantry and two regiments of cavalry. However one of the battalions, Guise's 6th Foot, was garrisoning the various Highland forts and two companies of another, Lascelles 58th/47th Foot, were in Edinburgh Castle. It was also considered impractical to take the cavalry into the hills, so one regiment was left in Edinburgh and the other at Stirling. In the end Cope assembled only the ten companies of Murray's 57th/46th Foot, eight companies of Lascelles' 58th/47th, five companies of Lee's 55th/44th Foot and two Additional (or depot) companies of recruits for the 43rd/42nd Highlanders for his expedition. Guise's Foot had recently been rebuilt by recruiting in Warwickshire after a debilitating spell of duty in the West Indies while the other infantry units had largely been recruited in Scotland since the outbreak of war in 1743 – at least half the officers subsequently captured at Prestonpans would be Scots. None of them had seen action before.

Marching from Stirling on 20 August Cope hoped to augment this little force with substantial

## REGIMENTS

*Originally regiments were simply known by the name of their current colonel, but in the 1740s numbers were allocated to avoid confusion and denote their seniority. However in 1748 Oglethorpe's 42nd Foot, and ten regiments of Marines, which had ranked as the 44th to 53rd Foot were disbanded, which resulted in a number of regiments shuffling up in order of seniority. The Black Watch, originally numbered as the 43rd Foot, thus became the 42nd and Lascelles' 58th became the 47th Foot. Where a unit is assigned two numbers in the text, as in the 43rd/42nd or 58th/47th , the first represents the one which it actually bore during the Rising and the second is the one which it adopted after 1748.*

*The monument to the battle, placed fairly close to the position occupied by Cope's right flank.*

numbers of loyalist volunteers, but all he actually succeeded in picking up en route was an incomplete company of recruits for the Earl of Loudon's embryonic 64th Highlanders. Nevertheless, he did at least have access to a very efficient intelligence network and at Dalwhinnie he received definite information that the rebels planned to fight him in the steep traverses of the Corryairack Pass. Judging the position too strong to be forced Cope abandoned his original intention of establishing a forward base at Fort Augustus, but recognising the political consequences of retreating, he instead marched north along the line of the present A9 to Inverness.

Exactly what he hoped to achieve by this is unclear, but at least having reached Inverness Cope was at last joined by some useful reinforcements. He had already taken a company of Guise's 6th Foot from Ruthven Barracks near Kingussie, now he found another in Inverness, together with three more incomplete companies of the 64th Highlanders and a 200-strong loyalist battalion raised by Captain George Monro of Culcairn. Only too well aware of the fact that by avoiding contact with the rebels he had uncovered the road to the south, he then marched hard for Aberdeen, embarked his forces on ships there and arrived off Dunbar on 17

*Senior Highland officer as depicted by McIan.*

September. He was just twenty-four hours too late to save Edinburgh.

In the meantime, disappointed in their hope that the general would obligingly march into the trap prepared for him at Corryairack, the rebels' immediate reaction was to follow Cope to Inverness, but eventually the temptation of marching on Edinburgh proved too much. Masking the move with an unsuccessful attack on Ruthven Barracks on 29 August – it was held by just twelve men under Sergeant Terry Molloy – they moved south and occupied Perth on 3 September. After resting up for a week they crossed the Forth by the Fords of Frew, eight miles above Stirling Castle, on 13 September. No attempt was made or indeed could be made to stop them there and the single regiment of cavalry set to watching the crossings – Colonel James Gardiner's 13th Dragoons – fell back on Edinburgh.

There the rebels' approach was viewed with increasing concern. Although the burgh was still largely surrounded by the Flodden Wall it was rightly reckoned to be indefensible, and to make matters worse there were strong suspicions that the Lord Provost, Archibald Stewart, was a closet Jacobite. Whatever his true sympathies he was certainly in a difficult position for Cope's march northwards had left Edinburgh undefended save by the tiny garrison in the castle and by the 14th Dragoons. This regiment's tactical repertoire was limited to a panic stricken flight to the rear every time an enemy was rumoured to be approaching. Nevertheless when letters of service arrived from the Government on 9 September authorising the raising of a Loyalist corps, to be called the Edinburgh Regiment, Stewart oversaw the recruitment of 200 men within a week. Another 400 men were also mustered into the part-time Edinburgh Volunteers although their services were to be limited to patrolling the streets in conjunction with the existing City Guard.

By 15 September Colonel Gardiner and his 13th Dragoons had fallen back on Edinburgh and were joined at Corstorphine by the 14th Dragoons and the newly-raised Edinburgh Regiment. There Gardiner was superseded by a brigadier, Thomas Fowke, who had just arrived from Berwick. The colonel at this point was apparently suffering from a bad cold and gladly turned over command, but the gallant brigadier, deciding that cavalry were of no use in defending a town, immediately decided to abandon the capital and retreat to Dunbar. No sooner had he gone than the rebels turned up and in rather mysterious circumstances seized Edinburgh without any resistance on the night of 17/18 September.

Undaunted by this unwelcome news, Cope duly landed and marched westwards from Dunbar on the morning of 19 September with the intention of retaking the capital. However next day a reconnaissance party led by the Earl of Loudon discovered that the rebels were themselves marching out to meet him. At the time Cope's men were standing on a flat, stubble-covered 'extensive corn field, plain and level, without a bush or tree' close by the village of Prestonpans, and, as luck would have it immediately adjacent to Colonel Gardiner's house. As Cope's ADC, Captain James Forbes described it, it appeared to be an ideal battle ground:

> The Field which the General Drew up in was about an English Mile Square, where both Dragoons and Foot Could Act; and very well Secur'd on all Sides to prevent any Surprize; when we first Drew up the Front of the Army pointed South

*The waggonway, looking north. Cope's army was drawn up along it on the left.*

*The view from the waggonway towards the Jacobite front line, not improbably marked by the line of trees.*

*The view from the waggonway back across the field in which Cope's army was drawn up.*

west, the village of Prestonpans and the Defiles Leading to it, and Colonel Gardiner's House in our Front; The Town of Tranent with a Great many Coal Pits, Hedges and Ditches on our Left Flank; Seaton House and a Narrow Defile Leading from Haddington in our Rear, and the Sea with the Village Cockenny [Cockenzie] on our Right Flank.

The rebels also thought it was a good position and what started off as a bold advance turned into a black comedy. In large part the ensuing farce was a reflection of the rebels' chaotic command structure. The titular head of the Jacobite army was of course Prince Charles Edward Stuart but he was, quite literally, no more than a figurehead and the day to day administration of the army fell to the Adjutant and Quartermaster General, Colonel John Sullivan. Far from being the incompetent buffoon of popular legend, the forty-five-year-old Irishman was in fact a very capable professional soldier, who had learned his trade in the French Army and quite unusually had experience of both staff work and irregular warfare. Unfortunately however, like many professional soldiers, he had little time for enthusiastic amateurs and chief amongst those amateurs was Lord George Murray.

A younger brother of the Duke of Atholl, Murray's background excited suspicion from the very beginning. Born in 1694 he had thrown up a regular commission as an ensign in the Royal Scots to join the Jacobites in 1715. He also fought at Glenshiel in 1719 but he was pardoned in 1726 and then in 1745 unsuccessfully tried to raise some loyalist volunteers for Sir John Cope's army. His defection to the rebels at Perth came rather late in the day and although he was at once appointed a lieutenant general in recognition of his supposed local influence, many of his colleagues regarded him with considerable wariness. Nor did his arrogant manner endear him to many and one of his own staff officers, named James Johnstone, candidly summed him up as:

> vigilant, active and diligent; his plans were always judiciously formed, and he carried them promptly and vigorously into execution. However, with an infinity of good qualities, he was not without his defects: proud, haughty, blunt and imperious, he wished to have the exclusive disposal of everything and, feeling his superiority, would listen to no advice.

Now, finding Cope's army very strongly posted, Murray argued that a frontal attack was out of the question and declaring himself well acquainted with the area, proceeded to lead the rebel army up on to the commanding height of Falside Hill, to the south. So far so good, but having gained that position, just to the west of the village of Tranent, it soon turned out that Murray's knowledge of the area was not quite so extensive as he claimed. When taking a closer look the rebel commanders discovered to their dismay that a long narrow strip of bogland known as the Tranent Meadows lay at the foot of the hill, which would effectively stop any Highland charge in its tracks. As Johnstone ruefully commented:

> We arrived, about two o'clock in the afternoon, within musket shot of the enemy, where we halted behind an eminence, having a full view of the camp of General Cope, the position of which was chosen with a great deal of skill. The more we examined it, the more we were convinced of the impossibility of attacking it; and we were all thrown into consternation, and quite a loss what course to take... we spent the afternoon in reconnoitring this position; the more we examined it, the more our uneasiness and chagrin increased, as we saw no possibility of attacking it without exposing ourselves to be cut to pieces in a disgraceful manner.

As another eyewitness, named Henderson, very succinctly put it, 'This was not a proper situation for Highlanders, for they must have nothing before them that can hinder them to run at the enemy'. Not surprisingly the rebels soon began to fall out amongst themselves, but, in the meantime, Colonel Sullivan very properly took a number steps to ensure the security of the army. First he placed an outpost of some 50 men from Cameron of Locheil's Regiment in the churchyard at the bottom end of Tranent – 'for what reason' sneered Lord George Murray, 'I could not understand'. As events would show there was a great deal about soldiering which Murray did not understand and certainly, as another professional soldier, Sir John McDonnell commented, such outposts were 'the usual practice of infantry'. Indeed as the Jacobites would discover to their cost, Cope had also covered his own position with a number of similar outposts.

At any rate, having secured the churchyard, Sullivan next posted two battalions of the Atholl Brigade to cover the roads leading to Edinburgh and Musselburgh

Cockenzie

The Waggonway with Cope's Army drawn up along it.

*Prestonpans battlefield as seen from the Meadowmill mound. Although at first sight intrusive the power-lines and other modern features reflect the semi-industrial character of the original field. The dark line crossing the fields on the right is the waggonway used to align Cope's army as it formed up in the dawn.*

just in case Cope should attempt to slip past the Jacobites under cover of darkness. This immediately precipitated a furious row with Murray, who was outraged that they had been moved without consulting him, although by his own admission he had himself just taken advantage of Sullivan's absence to withdraw the outpost from the churchyard.

Ostensibly he had done so because it was coming under fire, but the real reason was that without consulting anybody else he had decided to move to another position and launch an attack on Cope's army from the east. Accordingly he began marching the rebel army around to the other side of Tranent and when Sullivan expostulated with him, blithely announced that 'it was not possible to attack the enemy on the west side of the village, that the men he had placed at the foot [in the churchyard] were exposed to no purpose; and that as there were exceeding good fields on the east side for the men to lie well and safe all that night, I should satisfy his Royal Highness how easy it would be to attack the enemy by the east side'.

In the circumstances this was probably the best course of action open to the Jacobites, but it was hardly sensible to advertise their intentions by moving into position in broad daylight. Naturally, more recriminations followed but the end result was that the army, now once again concentrated on top of the hill remained where it was until nightfall. In the meantime it was agreed to fall in with Murray's proposal to march eastwards, fetch a compass around the far end of the Tranent

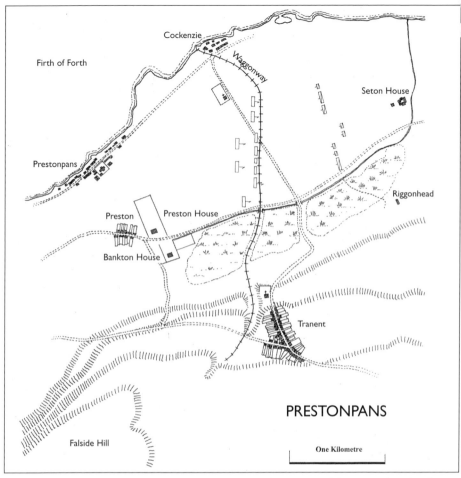

**PRESTONPANS**

Cockenzie

Firth of Forth

Waggonway

Seton House

Prestonpans

Riggonhead

Preston

Preston House

Bankton House

Tranent

Falside Hill

One Kilometre

*Initial dispositions at outset of battle. Cope's artillery was placed in a single battery on the right of his infantry line. His baggage and the Highland companies guarding it was in the churchyard at Cockenzie, to the rear of Hamilton's 14th Dragoons.*

Meadows and then attack Cope across the open cornfields. Interestingly, in the light of some of the criticism which would later be levelled against the choice of battlefield at Culloden seven months later, it is perhaps worth emphasising that they were committing themselves to a frontal attack across ground which was flatter and far more exposed than Culloden Moor, and that they would be attacking a foe who had a higher proportion of cavalry and artillery than the Duke of Cumberland would then enjoy. Yet none of the Jacobite memoirs betray any uneasiness at this prospect, for on the contrary as Henderson explicitly pointed out, the flat and unobstructed field of stubble was also ideal for a Highland charge.

At any rate they duly set off into the night only to have any chance of surprise completely scuppered when every dog in Tranent commenced a furious barking and alerted Cope's officers to the fact that something was going on. Notwithstanding the words of the famous song, the general was far from asleep and indeed had spent a very wearisome day reacting to every move the rebels made. Initially he drew up his men facing westwards towards Edinburgh, then redeployed them to meet the threatened attack from Falside Hill to the south. Shortly afterwards, in response to Sullivan's posting the Atholl Brigade astride the Musselburgh road, he again deployed them facing west, this time parallel with but a little forward from his original position. Then of course the rebels moved around to the east side of Tranent and so he again drew up his army facing southwards across the Tranent Meadows, pushed out his picquets and set large watchfires across his front. Now as the barking died down the soldiers stood to their arms and peered into the misty darkness in anticipation of an attack.

At first they waited in vain. Shortly before the rebels moved off from Tranent a local volunteer named Robert Anderson had offered to lead them by way of a shortcut along a narrow wildfowler's path which ran directly across the meadows close by Riggonhead Farm, instead of looping the long way around the end of them. Unexpectedly however, as they stole forward in the pre-dawn darkness they found it covered by a picquet of dragoons – the dragoons' commander, Colonel James Gardiner, was himself a local man and just as familiar with the path as Anderson.

Finding the rebels coming down the path towards them, the dragoons very properly fired off their muskets or pistols and then swiftly retired to give the alarm. Cope and his men were thereby alerted in good time to both the imminence and the direction of the rebel assault, and granted precious minutes to redeploy for the fourth and last time, facing eastwards. Given the low standard of training enjoyed by his raw recruits and the fact that it was still dark this was a creditable enough achievement in itself, although the deployment must have been considerably assisted by the existence of the Seton Waggonway, a colliery railway which traversed the battlefield more or less on a north-south alignment. In swinging the army around in the dark it was only necessary for Cope to order his regiments to line up along this railway in order to face the rebels in good order.

According to the well-informed *Scots Magazine* he had a total of 2,191 men that morning, exclusive of officers, sergeants and drummers. On the other hand Cope's transport officer reckoned there were only 1,467 infantrymen landed at Dunbar, to which were added 567 troopers belonging to the two dragoon regiments. This produces a total of

## MUSKETS

British soldiers were primarily armed with the Land Pattern Firelock with a 46" long barrel of 12 bore, .75 calibre, while Dragoons had carbines with 42" long barrels. The latter term is today used for a much short-barrelled weapon, but in the eighteenth century it was a very specific term used for weapons of 16 bore, .69 calibre. Initially Jacobite muskets were a mixture of sporting guns and a few military ones left over from previous affairs, but after Prestonpans two regiments, Ogilvy's and Glenbuchat's, were completely armed with firelocks taken from Cope's men. Thereafter however as arms shipments were run through the blockade they were able to achieve a fair degree of standardisation in equipping themselves with French military muskets, or a very similar Spanish copy, both of which were 16 bore.

only 2,034 rank and file, which may either mean that the *Scots Magazine* total did include the officers, or that it included the sea-gunners and about eighty-odd Loyalist volunteers from Edinburgh, few of whom were actually present when the battle began. Moreover 233 men, including all five companies of the 43rd/42nd and 64th Highlanders were detached to Cockenzie to act as a baggage guard. All in all therefore at dawn on 21 September Cope's main battle line can only have mustered 1,234 bayonets and 567 cavalry troopers.

On the left was Hamilton's 14th Dragoons, commanded by Lieutenant Colonel William Wright, with two squadrons in the front line and a third in reserve. Well aware that the rebels had no cavalry to speak of, Cope ordered both Hamilton's and Gardiner's Regiments to draw up two ranks deep, rather than the usual three in order to make the most of his superiority in this arm.

Next came Murray's 57th/46th Foot, commanded by Lieutenant Colonel Jasper Clayton, then a composite battalion commanded by Major John Severn comprising eight companies of Lascelles' 58th/47th and the two companies of Guise's 6th taken from the Highland garrisons. The main infantry battle line was completed by the half battalion of Lee's 55th/44th on the right under Lieutenant Colonel Peter Halkett, and a detachment of 136 men under Captain Robert Blake. The latter had formed the outer picquets during the night and in the hurry of forming the battle line it was thought expedient to form them up in an *ad hoc* little battalion by themselves rather than disrupt the deployment of their parent units.

On the right wing proper were six light curricle guns – artillery mounted on light carts or curricles whose shafts doubled as the trail when the horse had been unhitched – and four small Coehorn mortars manned by a rather scratch crew of volunteer officers and sea-gunners. These were backed up by an artillery guard of 100 men under Captain John Cochrane, which was again drawn from the infantry battalions. Finally the three squadrons of Gardiner's 13th Dragoons. Unfortunately there was only enough room to deploy a single squadron of dragoons, commanded by Lieutenant Colonel Shugborough Whitney on the extreme right of the front line. A second squadron under Gardiner himself was posted behind the guns and the third stood in reserve.

They did not have long to wait in this position and a loyalist volunteer named John Home recalled that, 'Harvest was just

*Highland gentleman, identified by the Penicuik artist as MacGregor of Dalnasplutrach.*

got in, and the ground was covered with a thick stubble, which rustled under the feet of the Highlanders as they ran on, speaking and muttering in a manner that expressed and heightened their fierceness and rage. When they set out the mist was very thick; but before they had got half-way, the sun rose, dispelled the mist, and showed the armies to each other'. What it also showed was that, in contrast to Cope's men, the rebels had made a mess of their deployment.

Although the Jacobites were rather less punctilious than their opponents in recording the numbers of men in each regiment present and fit for duty each morning, there is no doubt that with something over 2,200 men they outnumbered Cope's forces. Indeed in infantry they outnumbered the regulars by nearly two to one, albeit they had only thirty-six cavalrymen to oppose Cope's 567 dragoons.

Their front line comprised two brigades or wings, the right commanded by the Duke of Perth comprised three battalions of MacDonalds under Clanranald, Glengarry and Keppoch. The first and last both numbered a little over 200 men, while Glengarry's which had been reinforced the day before by Grant of Sheuglie's sons with the Glen Urquhart and Glenmoriston men, had as many as 400.

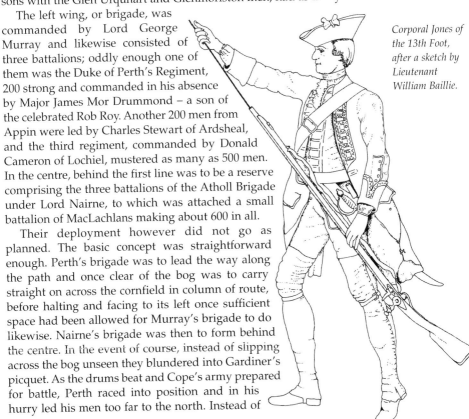

*Corporal Jones of the 13th Foot, after a sketch by Lieutenant William Baillie.*

The left wing, or brigade, was commanded by Lord George Murray and likewise consisted of three battalions; oddly enough one of them was the Duke of Perth's Regiment, 200 strong and commanded in his absence by Major James Mor Drummond – a son of the celebrated Rob Roy. Another 200 men from Appin were led by Charles Stewart of Ardsheal, and the third regiment, commanded by Donald Cameron of Lochiel, mustered as many as 500 men. In the centre, behind the first line was to be a reserve comprising the three battalions of the Atholl Brigade under Lord Nairne, to which was attached a small battalion of MacLachlans making about 600 in all.

Their deployment however did not go as planned. The basic concept was straightforward enough. Perth's brigade was to lead the way along the path and once clear of the bog was to carry straight on across the cornfield in column of route, before halting and facing to its left once sufficient space had been allowed for Murray's brigade to do likewise. Nairne's brigade was then to form behind the centre. In the event of course, instead of slipping across the bog unseen they blundered into Gardiner's picquet. As the drums beat and Cope's army prepared for battle, Perth raced into position and in his hurry led his men too far to the north. Instead of

*Colonel Gardiner's house, known at the time as Olive Stob it has since been renamed Bankton House.*

maintaining contact with him Murray on the other hand halted and faced as soon as his last regiment, Lochiel's, had cleared the bog.

The result was a yawning gap between the two brigades. Had they remained in that position it might have been plugged by bringing forward the reserve, but instead it would appear that as soon as Murray's brigade halted and fronted, he led it straight forward and, hearing the roar, Perth set off moments after him.

As the mist cleared it became all to obvious that whilst Perth's brigade was opposite and was outflanking Hamilton's Dragoons, and Murray's brigade was bearing down on Gardiner's Dragoons and the ragbag collection of artillery and *ad hoc* infantry detachments making up Cope's right, there was apparently nothing in front of the infantry.

Murray's 900 men made contact first. In the confusion as the army swung round to line up along the colliery railway, the sea-gunners had deserted, leaving just two officers and four men to man the artillery. As the Highlanders charged, the remaining four also took to their heels but at least the guns were loaded and Lieutenant Colonel Whitefoord and Major Griffith managed to fire them off. Cochrane's artillery guard, who must have been feeling very isolated, also 'gave a very irregular fire; and by falling back broke the Squadron of Colonel Gardiners that was in the rear'. Worse still, when Lieutenant Colonel Whitney tried to lead his squadron forward, the men first hesitated and then bolted, carrying the rest of the regiment with them – and all before the rebels even reached their position.

Virtually the same thing happened on the other flank. Outnumbered by more than three to one, the two squadrons of Hamilton's Dragoons made no attempt to charge the oncoming MacDonald regiments, but remained standing still until 'a few dropping shots' wounded both the commanding officer, Lieutenant Colonel Wright, and his second in command, Major Bowles. This was taken as the signal for their usual panic-stricken flight to the rear and although Captain Clark, commanding the reserve squadron, shouted to his men to stand fast in the hope that he could mount a charge as soon as the fugitives cleared his front, they too joined in the rout.

Unsurprisingly at this point Lord Drummore, a judge who was present as an interested spectator, 'concluded that all was lost and that it was full time for a Pen-and-Ink Gentleman to provide for his Safety'. Which, as he dryly observed to the subsequent court of inquiry, he did 'by riding off, but I hope with more Discretion and Deliberation than the Dragoons did'.

Naturally enough some of the Highlanders rushed off in pursuit of the fleeing dragoons, but others turned to deadlier work. Thus far untroubled by anyone Cope's infantry had maintained their position along the railway line, but now a

*Monument to Colonel James Gardiner of the 13th Dragoons, killed in his own garden.*

Gardiner's house

Meadowmill

*'Johnnie Cope's Road' up Birsley Brae, so called because Cope retreated along it with what remained of his army. Colonel Gardiner's house can be seen in middle distance on the left, and the Meadowmill mound just above the traffic sign on the right.*

party of Locheil's Camerons and some others of Lord George Murray's brigade began rolling up their right flank. As Major John Severn of Lascelles' afterwards testified, 'A large Body of their Left rush'd on obliquely on our Right Flank, and broke the Foot as it were by Platoons, with so rapid a Motion, that the whole Line was broken in a few Minutes'.

Severn's commanding officer, Colonel Lascelles, suddenly found himself confronted by a party of Highlanders who demanded his surrender, but no sooner had he handed over his sword than they rushed off again. Instead of running to the rear Lascelles then very sensibly headed eastwards, so that he 'unexpectedly escaped to Seaton, between the Remainder of the left Column of the Rebels, and that next to it, which were at a considerable distance from one another'. This interesting comment underlines the point that the victory was so swift the Jacobite reserve had still not caught up.

There was still some mopping up to be done. Abandoned by his dragoons, Colonel Gardiner tried to rally some of the infantry but was knocked down by a Highlander wielding a Lochaber Axe, and quite literally fell dying in his own garden. Nearby, a Fifeshire laird, Lieutenant Colonel Peter Halkett made a stand with fourteen of his men outside the house, but Lord George Murray brought up 100 or so rebels and politely invited him to surrender. Similarly the Highland Companies at Cockenzie surrendered after firing a single token volley. This was probably the last organised resistance. Lord Home, a Scots Guards officer, did succeed in rallying some of the dragoons at pistol-point but recognising there was no hope of getting them to fight, Cope led them off the field by a lane just to the west of Bankton House, afterwards known as 'Johnnie Cope's Road'.

The entire battle had lasted no more than seven or eight minutes and in that time the British Army lost some 150 dead and 1,326 prisoners, while the Rebels on the other hand admitted to five officers and thirty men killed and another seventy or eighty wounded. It was by any accounting a famous victory, but like the battle of Kilsyth 100 years before it was far from being decisive. Nevertheless it fostered the notion that the Highland charge was irresistible and reinforced the Highland clansmen's reputation for merciless savagery.

# *Falkirk*

A fter Prestonpans Charles Edward held court at the house of his ancestors in Holyrood and behaved as though he was indeed Prince Regent of his father's ancient kingdom, but no-one was under any illusions that the campaign was over and eventually he and his advisers were faced with tough decisions.

It is important to appreciate that the Jacobites' position was far from secure. On the credit side they had defeated Cope's army, occupied Edinburgh and set up their own administration in much of eastern Scotland. As a direct result they gained hundreds of recruits and raised a number of new regiments, including some badly needed cavalry. Rather ominously, on the other hand, nearly all of those recruits were Lowlanders. In a report prepared by General Wade some years before the rising the Highlands were reckoned capable of producing as many as 30,000 fighting men. But, so far, barely a tenth of that number had rallied to the Prince's banner. Support for the Stuarts was far from universal in the Highlands but another, equally important, factor was that with the exception of the tiny barracks at Inversnaid the rebels had not captured a single garrison or fortress. On the contrary the regulars holding those posts – and in particular Inverness – not only hindered Jacobite recruiting in the Highlands, but also encouraged and assisted in the raising of what eventually grew into quite substantial Loyalist forces.

Ideally the Jacobites' first priority should have been the capture of these castles and forts and the consolidation of their embryonic regime in order to establish and afterwards defend an independent Scotland. Unfortunately, even if Prince Charles

*Scots Loyalist volunteer as depicted by the Penicuik artist.*

Edward had not been so obsessed with recovering the English throne, the external threat was far too urgent to be ignored. Cope's army had been little more than a reinforced brigade largely made up of raw recruits. However over the border at Newcastle Field Marshal George Wade was overseeing a much more formidable concentration of veteran troops recalled from Flanders. Therefore whilst most of the rebels, committed as they were to a dissolution of the Union rather than a second restoration of the Stuarts, would have preferred to remain in Scotland, it was resolved to march south and seek a rapid and decisive resolution to the issue.

The march to Derby, and the successful retreat back to Scotland which followed was undoubtedly a notable undertaking. However admiration of its technical execution can all-too easily obscure its actual aims. When the rebel army marched out of Edinburgh on 31 October 1745 it still had no clear objective, but at Dalkeith two options were debated. The Prince favoured the direct approach of marching straight into Northumberland and bringing Wade to battle as soon as possible. With hindsight this was the only truly viable option open to the rebels, but even then the result was by no means certain.

In the end it was decided to avoid an immediate confrontation and instead to by-pass Wade and push south into Lancashire in the twin hopes of triggering both an English Jacobite uprising and the French intervention which was still considered as essential to their eventual success. Most of them were realistic enough to recognise that in the longer term they could not stand alone. This all-important point requires emphasising for although at Derby, Prince Charles Edward had convinced himself that London itself was within his grasp, the other Jacobite leaders had never contemplated seizing the largest city in Europe by themselves. This is starkly clear from Lord George Murray's intervention in the fateful meeting when the decision was taken to turn back:

Lord George told him [the Prince] that it was the opinion of Every body present that the Scots had now done all that could be Expected of them. That they had marched into the heart of England ready to join with any party that would declare for him, that none had, and that the Counties through which the Army had pass'd had Seemed much more Enemies than friends to his Cause, that there was no French Landed in England, and that if there was any party in England for him, it was very odd that they had never so much as Either sent him money or intelligence or the least advice what to do...

## HIGHLAND INDEPENDENT COMPANIES

*One of the biggest problems faced by the Jacobites was the degree of opposition which they faced in the Highlands. Several incomplete companies of the Earl of Loudoun's 64th Highlanders were scattered in various posts and provided a nucleus for the formation of a Loyalist army. At the end of October 1745, Major General John Campbell of Mamore was commissioned to raise 'eight Independent Companies each of 100 men with the proper officers; and likewise to arm 16 such companies more, without the charge of commissioned officers, who are to serve without pay and are to be raised from the Duke of Argyll's and the Earl of Breadalbane's Contrys'. These companies became known as the Argyle Militia and the eight regular companies together with a company from the Black Watch and two from Loudoun's 64th served at Falkirk and afterwards at Culloden. In addition a further eighteen Highland Independent Companies were raised in the north of Scotland by the Earl of Loudoun. It is worth noting that the companies were primarily employed in a counter-insurgency role and much of the harrying of the glens which followed Culloden was actually carried out by these Highlanders*

Suppose even the Army march'd on and beat the Duke of Cumberland yett in the Battle they must lose some men, and they had after the King's own army consisting of near 7000 men near London to deal with... that certainly 4,500 Scots had never thought of putting a King upon the English Throne by themselves.

Finding themselves unwanted in England the rebels returned to Scotland to face an interesting tactical situation. They had no sooner abandoned Edinburgh exactly two months before than it was re-occupied by an infantry brigade marched up from Berwick by Brigadier General Handasyde. Briefly appointed Commander-in-Chief North Britain, Handasyde was an energetic officer who quickly supplemented his regular battalions by re-constituting the Edinburgh Regiment, raising two more Loyalist volunteer battalions in Glasgow and Paisley and another in Stirling. Thus reinforced he was able to hold all

*William Boyd, Lord Kilmarnock, a Jacobite cavalry officer from Falkirk.*

the Forth Crossings and so prevent a second Jacobite army led by Lord John Drummond (who had recently landed at Montrose with two battalions of French troops) from marching south to reinforce the Prince's army.

In the event Drummond was forced to sit tight at Perth until the unexpected arrival of the Prince and his men at Glasgow rendered the continued defence of the Forth untenable.At that point the Loyalist brigade, commanded by the Earl of Home, retired with the regulars to Edinburgh and Drummond at last moved south.

By now it was January and the weather was becoming the dominant factor in determining strategy on both sides. The rebels retreat from Derby had been shadowed by King George's favourite son, the Duke of Cumberland, but having followed them as far as Carlisle, he was temporarily recalled to London. Instead Lieutenant General Henry Hawley was appointed Commander-in-Chief North Britain and sent northwards from Newcastle to finish them off. All-too often characterised as a brutal martinet of very limited ability, Hawley was in fact a capable officer and military theorist, but he was in his late 60s by 1746 and essentially cautious.

For now his first priority was to secure Edinburgh, but hampered by bad weather and a shortage of accommodation on the road he could only march up two battalions at a time and so did not complete his concentration there until 10 January. In the meantime the Jacobites decided to seize the strategically important town of Stirling, no doubt in the hope that by holding the Forth crossings, they could also hold the north of Scotland indefinitely. This proved to be far from easy. Embarrassingly, the rebels were initially defied not by regular soldiers, but by the burgh's loyalist militia who manned its crumbling walls against them. Then even after they eventually agreed to open the gates, the castle towering above the town still held out, forcing the Jacobites to embark on an inept and ultimately futile siege. Within the week Hawley was on the march.

Hearing that he was on the way, the Jacobites scaled down their siege and prepared to meet him on nearby Plean Moor. Unfortunately, the meeting was delayed, for Hawley, unwilling to patrol aggressively with his cavalry, moved forward very cautiously and encamped at Falkirk, where he was joined on 17 January by the Argyll Militia. This slow and methodical approach created a problem for the rebels. It was after all the middle of January and after forming in order of battle for two successive days they reluctantly accepted that the weather conditions made it quite impossible to keep the army concentrated in the open for any longer:

> The field that had been pitched upon was of no use now that Hawley was within six miles. As the Prince had no tents he could not keep his men together above four-and-twenty hours, and if Hawley did not come up in that time they must be sent back to their cantonments; in that case Hawley might beat up the quarters, one after another, and destroy the whole army without a battle.

In short, faced with the unpalatable prospect of dispersing again into their quarters and so running the danger of being cut up in detail if Hawley moved forward again unexpectedly, they took the soldier-like decision to go on to the offensive themselves. Three battalions under the Duke of Perth and old John Gordon of Glenbuchat were left behind to maintain the blockade of Stirling, whilst the greater part of the army, comprising what was now known as the Highland Division under Lord George Murray, and a number of Lowland units intended to form a second line, were committed to the operation. Murray proposed that they should begin by seizing the Hill of Falkirk, a bare open ridge on the south-west of the town, which overlooked Hawley's camp. Murray would cover the movement by indulging his penchant for elaborate diversionary movements and

*British grenadier 'charging his bayonet' after Lieutenant Baillie.*

set off due southwards, to cross Carron Water by the ford known as Dunipace Steps. Meanwhile, Lord John Drummond with the cavalry and a composite battalion of French regulars was ostentatiously sent off on a different route, down the east side of the Torwood towards Larbert.

So far so good. As intended, Drummond's men were spotted almost at once and Hawley's forces placed on the alert against a possible Jacobite advance down the main road, but for some reason it never occurred to the General to send some of his cavalry out to see exactly what was happening. When Drummond's men were then seen to turn west along Carron Water it was cheerfully assumed they had merely been on a reconnaissance and the regulars started to relax until a loyalist scout named Sprewel galloped into the camp at about one o'clock with the news that the rebels were crossing the Carron and closing fast.

As his army hurriedly formed up, Hawley, galloped straight up on to the hill and a desperate race began to secure the summit. One of his staff officers, James Mackenzie, was sent

*The monument to the battle on Falkirk Muir, close to Hawley's right wing.*

...to order the Cavalry to move that way immediately and the Infantry and Artillery to follow them as fast as possible, he [Hawley] being afraid the rebels might get by us on the left, and perhaps cut our communication with Edinburgh, or, at least, get away from us, which was the thing we were most afraid of'.

The rebels were already forming in order of battle. Their front line, from left to right, comprised Locheil's Camerons (800); Ardsheal's Appin Regiment (300); the Master of Lovat's Regiment (300); Lady Mackintosh's Regiment (200); Farquharson of Monaltrie's Regiment (150); Lord Cromartie's Regiment (200); Cluny's MacPhersons (300); and the three MacDonald regiments, Clanranald (350), Glengarry (800 in two battalions) and Keppoch (400). Behind them the second line comprised two battalions of Lord Lewis Gordon's Regiment (400), two battalions of Lord Ogilvy's Regiment (500), and the three battalions of the Atholl Brigade (600) which, like Gordon's and Ogilvy's men, was accounted a Lowland corps. It

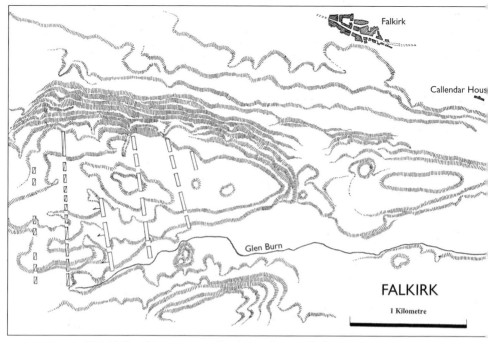

*Presumed initial dispositions at outset of battle. Note how Hawley's cavalry is forward of his infantry line, not formed on its left. The position of the Loyalist volunteers is unknown, but they appear to have been somewhere in the left rear. The Argyle Militia and Highland Independent Companies seem to have been left guarding the camp and did not take part in the battle.*

may have been intended that they should have been posted at wide intervals behind the first line, but there are indications that all three may have been bunched together behind the MacDonald regiments on the right. Trailing some way behind them came a notional third line comprising the cavalry under Sir John McDonnell and a composite infantry battalion of about 250 regulars belonging to two companies of the blue-jacketed Royal Ecossois and three of the red-coated Irish Picquets under Lord John Drummond. All of these figures are round ones and perhaps in some cases rather too optimistic, but in total the Jacobite army appears to have numbered something in the region of 5,750 infantry and 360 cavalry, of whom about 3,800 were the clansmen in the front line.

This time the battlefield they were approaching was to conform much more closely to the popular expectations. From the outskirts of the town the hill rose steeply up to a bleak moorland plateau. There were a few small farms, or rather steadings, surrounded by walled enclosures, but for the most part it was an undulating area of common grazing land. It was also quite rough and about halfway up the hill the slope was cut by a deep ravine, which would have a significant effect on the course of the battle.

In response to Hawley's summons his cavalry turned to their left, crossed the Stirling road and set off along a lane known as 'Maggie Wood's Loan' which led them out on to the open hillside. He had three regiments commanded by Colonel

*The head of the ravine which covered Hawley's right wing. It is now choked with trees although it is uncertain to what extent the north side of the hill was covered in woodland in 1746. Most accounts suggest it was quite bare.*

Francis Ligonier, a very promising young officer who had succeeded the slain Gardiner in command of the 13th Dragoons. As the brigade formed up, the 13th Dragoons were on the left, Cobham's 10th Dragoons were in the centre, and Hamilton's 14th Dragoons on the right. Ordinarily, as the senior regiment, Cobham's should have been posted on the right, but as both the 13th and 14th had run away at Prestonpans and were generally regarded as unreliable it was no doubt considered that the 10th Dragoons would be best placed in the centre of the

*These scruffy vagabonds are in fact British regulars sketched by the Penicuik artist on their way to Falkirk in January 1746.*

*A modern re-enactment showing a company of British regulars drawn up on Falkirk Muir.*

brigade. In any case with some 300 men in the ranks it was also stronger than the other two who mustered only 519 troopers between them.

Further down the hill and as yet unconvinced of the urgency of the situation, a rather disgruntled Brigadier Cholmondley described the tribulations of Hawley's infantry:

> The Army was immediately order'd to stand to their Arms, and form, in front of their incampment. All the Cavalry were order'd to march to the Left, to take post there, and the two Lines of Infantry were order'd to face to the Left, and in this Position, we march'd to the Left near half a mile, but as we had hollow roads, and very uneven Ground to pass, we were in great Confusion. Here we form'd again, in my Opinion a very good Situation, but we were no sooner form'd but order'd a second time, to take Ground to the Left, and as we march'd, all the way up hill, and Over very uneven Ground, our men were greatly blown.

They were formed in two lines. The first comprised Edward Wolfe's 8th Foot,

Cholmondley's 34th, Pulteney's 13th, the second battalion of the 1st (Royal) Regiment – the Royal Scots – Price's 14th Foot and Ligonier's 59th/48th Foot. The second line was made up of Blakeney's 27th Foot, Monro's 37th, Fleming's 36th, Barrell's 4th and Battereau's 62nd, with Howard's 3rd Foot (the Buffs) forming a sort of reserve. In all, Hawley had 5,488 regular infantry in addition to his 819 cavalry. He also had a substantial number of Loyalist troops. The Earl of Home had a little brigade formed of the Glasgow and Paisley regiments, which together with an Edinburgh company and some of the Stirling volunteers, numbered about 700 men, while Lieutenant Colonel 'Jack' Campbell of Mamore had four regular companies from the 43rd/42nd (Black Watch) and 64th Highlanders, and twelve companies of the Argyll Militia totalling some 800 in all. Both Loyalist formations were posted at the bottom of the hill and would play little part in the coming fight, while Hawley's artillery – ten guns – would never come into action at all.

About 3.30 or 4.00pm Hawley ordered Ligonier forward against the approaching MacDonalds. He was of course taking a risk in ordering them to attack without either preparation or support, but there was no other way to prevent the enemy from getting on top of the hill before his own infantry. In any case his experiences at Sheriffmuir 30 years before, where he had led Evans' Dragoons, had convinced him that the Highlanders would not stand and, as James Mackenzie related afterwards, 'as the General imagined the enemy was more afraid of horse than foot, he ordered the dragoons to begin the attack'.

Until the dragoons came over the crest, the rebels were seemingly unaware that their opponents were simultaneously hurrying up the other side of the hill and as some of them afterwards admitted, the cavalry's unexpected appearance caused

*More Scots Loyalist volunteers sketched by the Penicuik artist.*

*The Jacobite reserve comprised a provisional battalion of French regulars made up of three companies of Irish troops dressed like these in red coats, and two companies of the Royal Ecossois dressed in shorter blue jackets with red cuffs, and blue bonnets instead of hats.*

considerable dismay. Some accounts suggest that the Jacobites held their fire until the dragoons came within a few yards, but in fact as soon as they came in sight the Jacobite front rank immediately fired a hasty volley at long range, seemingly without doing any damage. However another volley delivered by the second rank at point blank range was much more effective and a loyalist volunteer named Corse recalled that 'in one part of them [the dragoons] nearest us I saw day light through them in several places'. Just how many were shot down is uncertain. Cobham's, which went into the fight with about 300 men, had 276 at Culloden so probably lost no more than about 20 killed and wounded. No comparable figures are available for the other regiments but numbered among the dead was Lieutenant Colonel Whitney of the 13th Dragoons. Having thus been shot up – and almost certainly lost more horses than men – the greater part of his regiment, together with many of Cobham's 10th swerved aside and galloped off to the north between the two armies. Nevertheless a substantial number pressed on, and

> rushed upon the Highlanders at a hard trot, breaking their ranks, throwing down everything before them, and trampling the Highlanders under the feet of their horses. The most singular and extraordinary combat immediately followed. The Highlanders, stretched on the ground, thrust their dirks into the bellies of the horses. Some seized the riders by their clothes, dragged them down, and stabbed them with their dirks; several again used their pistols; but few of them had sufficient space to handle their swords.

They were in the end repulsed, but not before some of the dragoons broke right through the MacDonalds' ranks to attack Lord Ogilvy's men in the second line, who promptly threw down their colours and ran away. In the meantime Hamilton's 14th Dragoons had simply turned around and bolted straight back down their side of the hill. In the process, as Corse complained, they rode over the loyalist Glasgow Volunteers '... & carry'd off about a Company of our people; among whom I was, & would then have given my life for a shilling. Some of us they rode over, and some of us ran and rode so well that we got quit of them in about 5 or 600 yards, with the utmost difficulty'. Not all of the Glasgow men ran though, and some of them actually fired a volley into the panic-stricken dragoons, emptying a few more saddles.

No sooner had the dragoons been beaten off by both rebels and loyalists than the four MacDonald battalions scattered in pursuit and at the same time the rest of the rebel front line surged forward with them. In a moment of quite unbelievable drama, just as they came flooding over the crest a wild storm broke over them, blowing hard in the faces of Hawley's infantry still toiling up the hill. In the circumstances it is perhaps hardly surprising that many of the redcoats panicked and ran without firing a shot. To all appearances as the rest of the front line flooded down the hill in the MacDonalds' wake, it seemed the Jacobites were on the point of winning another famous victory. However two factors came into play against them.

In the first place, blind to each other's positions as they climbed the hill, the two armies were misaligned and while the MacDonalds and Locheil's Camerons outflanked Hawley's left, the British right wing similarly outflanked the Jacobite left. Moreover it was very securely protected by the ravine cutting across the hillside, which also very effectively funnelled the Jacobites over to their right and encouraged them to follow the victorious MacDonalds rather than tackle the formed units to their front. Of itself this need not necessarily have proved fatal, but the rebels' chaotic, or rather non-existent, command structure ultimately proved their undoing.

With the Duke of Perth left behind at Stirling, Lieutenant General Lord George Murray was the ranking officer on the field and as such should at the very least have taken overall charge of the first line, yet instead he chose to stand with the MacDonald brigade on the right. Why he did so is unclear, but the MacDonalds had no love for him and he may have felt his presence necessary to ensure that they obeyed him. If so he was sadly disappointed for they disregarded all his appeals to stand fast after repulsing the dragoons. Whatever the true state of affairs it is all too clear that no-one in the front line of the Jacobite Army was exercising any meaningful command above regimental level.

This was particularly unfortunate for it quickly became obvious that the initial success was more apparent than real. It was only the outflanked regiments of Hawley's left wing – Edward Wolfe's 8th; Blakeney's 27th and Monro's 37th – which actually broke and so suffered the heaviest casualties. A number of the regiments in the centre, including the Royals, also retired with indecent haste, but must have preserved their order as they fell back, for they were pretty well left alone and soon recovered their composure at the bottom of the hill. The Edinburgh Volunteers stood fast as well, and in one of the few glimpses of Hawley during this stage of the battle their captain, John Home, recorded how, after he rather tactlessly asked if any regiments were still standing, the general ordered him to get his men into an adjacent cattle fold.

There was certainly wild confusion on the lower slopes of the hill as Hawley's men tumbled back, but the Jacobites were incapable of exploiting it and in the midst of it all Brigadier General James Cholmondley ordered Barrell's 4th Foot and Ligonier's 59th/48th Foot to swing backwards and pour a succession of volleys into the rebels' exposed flank.

This brought about an immediate and dramatic change of fortunes: 'Mr John Roy Stuart, an officer in the service of France, afraid that this might be an ambuscade laid for us by the English, called out to the Highlanders to stop their pursuit, and the cry of stop flew immediately from rank to rank and threw the whole army into disorder'. Amidst the customary cries of treachery a great many Jacobites not only halted but ran away in their turn. As Colonel Sullivan disgustedly recalled

> ... the cursed hollow square came up, took our left in flanc & obliged them to retire in disorder. There was no remedy nor succor to be given them. The second ligne, yt HRHs counted upon, went off, past the river & some of them even went to Bannockburn, & Sterling, where they gave out yt we lost the day.

The rebels very nearly did, for not only had half of the front line and greater part of the second line run away, but the intrepid Brigadier Cholmondley was organising a counter-attack:

> During this time General Huske was rallying the other troops that had been broke, then I told these two battalions that if they would keep their ground, I would go back and rally the dragoons, they promised they would, and kept their word. Accordingly I went to the dragoons and rallied about one hundred of them, and told them I had repulsed the enemy with two weak battalions, and that if they would march up I would head them, and that I would order the two battalions to march up briskly at the same time, and give them their

*The tower of St Ninians kirk.*

This historic building which saw the Earl of Moray's division go out to fight Clifford's men at Bannockburn, was used by the Jacobites as a powder magazine and blown up as they retreated after the battle of Falkirk. Only the tower remained.

fire, and that they should fall in sword in hand. They were greatly pleased with this, and, with many oaths and Irish exclamations, they swore they would follow me. I marched them up to the two battalions, but when we were to advance they kept at least one hundred yards behind me; with some difficulty I got them to the top of the hill, where I saw the Highlanders formed behind some houses and a barn (I was forced to fire a pistol amongst them, before I could get them to do this), I then returned to the two battalions to march them up, here General Huske joined me, and I told him, that if we could get some more battalions to join us, we might drive them.

Just what Major General John Huske thought of Cholmondley's notions of maintaining discipline is not recorded, but although he had managed to bring up a further three battalions – Howard's 3rd, Price's 14th and Fleming's 36th Foot – he was less than keen on counter-attacking in the failing light and ordered him to withdraw.

Indeed by this point it was becoming difficult to actually find any formed bodies of rebel troops to fight. Lord George Murray, complaining he could find no pipers, was having no success whatever in recalling the MacDonalds, but Sir John McDonnell, having 'quitted the cavalry which would not listen to orders' helped Colonel Sullivan to rally some of the runaways at the Carron and then lead them back into the fight. Sullivan, who was doing more than anyone else to direct the battle, also managed to bring up the Irish Picquets, who by this time were the only formed body of Jacobites still on the field. With both darkness and heavy rain falling, and no real sign of the opposing army, Huske prudently declined to engage this little battalion and instead retired back to the camp.

For a time Hawley considered holding his position there, for by now he and Mordaunt had rallied most of his runaways. However although their men had been halted and formed in ranks again they were still pretty demoralised and in the darkness and driving rain no-one had much stomach for it. One of his officers glossed over the situation by writing that

> The weather was so severe that he [Hawley] chose rather to abandon his camp, and retire to Linlithgow, than to destroy the Men by lying on their Arms all Night, wet to the Skin, subject to continuall Alarms.

Unpalatable though it may have seemed, the decision to break contact was probably a sensible one but once arrived at Linlithgow it was soon found that all the ammunition remaining in the soldiers' cartridge boxes was soaked and useless, and so the retreat continued all the way back to Edinburgh.

Initially the Jacobites also considered retiring:

> Most were of the opinion to retreat towards Dunnipace and the places adjacent, where the men might be covered, it being a prodigious rain; but Lord George Murray was absolutely for marching into the town... and concluded with Count Mercy's expression at the battle of Parma, that he would either lie in the town or in paradise.

With 'not above six or seven hundred men with him' (half of them being the French regulars), he very cautiously moved into Falkirk, only to find it empty of British troops apart from a few stragglers. This gave the Jacobites sufficient excuse to claim a famous victory, but in reality both the course of the battle and its eventual outcome were remarkably similar to Sheriffmuir in 1715, where it was famously said that 'We ran and they ran, and everybody ran away man'.

Neither side had suffered many casualties. The Jacobites admitted to some fifty killed and between sixty and eighty wounded, while the British Army apparently lost about seventy killed, although that included no fewer than twenty officers. Ominously rumours soon began to circulate that many of those officers were killed in cold blood, including Sir Robert Munro of Foulis, the colonel of the 37th Foot. He was initially wounded and was being treated by his brother, a surgeon, when both were murdered. Munro's case aside there may have been some exaggeration in these stories, but they were remembered three months later at Culloden. The unusually high proportion of officers killed, as everyone readily admitted, was down to their having been deserted by their men and most of the officer casualties belonged to the three regiments – Wolfe's 8th, Blakeney's 27th and Monro's 37th Foot – which were outflanked and broken by the Camerons and Stewarts.

Large numbers of officers and men on both sides had in fact simply scattered far and wide across the countryside, and particularly on the Jacobite side were afterwards slow to return to the colours. Consequently there was no pursuit by the rebels and no real elation at their pretended victory, instead they were racked by recrimination and even outright despair. By contrast while the British Army was under no illusions that it had won the battle, neither its officers nor its men considered themselves beaten. Instead, when dried out and resupplied, and provided with a new commander – the Duke of Cumberland – they marched westwards once again. This time the rebels declined to fight and instead retired northwards to that final reckoning on Culloden Moor.

# Medieval Battles

**Stirling Bridge** (OS Explorer 366)
A battlesite which has been almost completely built over without losing its essential character. The best starting point is the Abbey Craig at Causwayhead, and as its name indicates the very straight and surprisingly long road - the old A9 - linking it with Stirling very substantially follows the track of the original Causeway. The stone footbridge over the Forth, a short distance upstream from the modern road bridge, dates from the fifteenth century but appears to have been patterned quite closely on the original wooden structure both in size and appearance. It is very easy therefore to get a good sense of the battlefield, still dominated as it is by Stirling Castle.

➡ From Stirling Bridge it is easy to move straight to the Bannockburn battlefield by continuing along the A9 as far as St Ninians.

**Falkirk**
Whilst a visit to the battlefield of Stirling Bridge is both straightforward and fascinating. Looking for the scene of Wallace's debacle at Falkirk is anything but. As discussed in the main text, the site cannot be established with any confidence. A good case has been made for the hill-slope on the south side of Callendar Wood, now fairly substantially built over, but on balance it seems much more likely that the Scots were drawn up slightly further to the west, on the burgh muir of Falkirk – the site of the Jacobite battle in 1746, details of which are given in the last chapter.

    **Recommended reading:** Most coverage of Stirling Bridge takes the form of adulatory and sometimes quite fanciful biographies of William Wallace. A good but dated corrective is Evan Barron's *Scottish War of Independence* (1934) which primarily deals with the role of the Comyns, Morays and other northerners. A useful modern account is Pete Armstrong's *Stirling Bridge and Falkirk 1297-98* (Osprey 2003).

**Bannockburn** (OS Explorer 366)
A fairly complex site through a combination of modern buildings and a busy railway line.

➡ A good starting point is to follow the A872 Glasgow Road (the old Roman road) from St. Ninians to the well-signposted Bannockburn Heritage Centre. Maintained by the National Trust for Scotland and otherwise known as the Borestone site, this is a largely open area at what was the Entry to the New Park and the scene of the skirmish on the first day when Bruce slew de Bohun.

➡ **The second site** is the Dryfield. Unsignposted the only practical way to approach it is to return to St. Ninians and then take the A9 Bannockburn Road as far as Bannockburn High School. Cleared of trees and now either levelled or built on, this site is held by some historians to be the actual site of the fighting on the second day, but even the most cursory examination of the escarpment within Balquiderock Wood on the north-eastern edge of the site is sufficient to dispel this notion. It would not have been impossible to bring heavy cavalry up the slope, but the sheer effort of doing so would not have been overlooked by the chroniclers - and nor would the awful consequences of being tumbled back down it again in defeat. At the bottom of the slope the area where Bruce formed up his army after emerging from the wood is now built up and completely severed from the Carse of Balquiderock proper by the railway line.

➡ **The third site,** the Carse, where the battle was fought is once again completely unsignposted and under threat of development. It can only be approached by either the A905 directly from Stirling, or better still by the A91 which itself can be accessed either from the bottom of Balquiderock Wood (if on foot) or from the south-eastern end of Bannockburn Road. The eastern side of the Carse, where Edward Bruce's division fought, is the least changed since 1314, and in any event it is instructive to look back from the English point of view to appreciate the obstacle posed by the Balquiderock escarpment and the woods from which the Scots army emerged so unexpectedly that morning long ago.

**Recommended Reading:** A number of books have been published recently on Bannockburn, some good and one downright awful. The best is Peter Reese's *Bannockburn* (Edinburgh 2000), which firmly plumps for the Carse site, but although Pete Armstrong's *Bannockburn 1314* (Osprey 2002) rather inexplicably cleaves to the Dryfield site, it still provides a good clear account of the campaign. However General Sir Philip Christieson's account, contained in the current National Trust for Scotland brochure is still the most sensible and concise one.

### Pinkie (OS Explorer 350)
Pinkie is a surprisingly large battlefield, albeit badly cut up by the expansion of Musselburgh, the main East Coast railway line and the A1.

➡ The best way to approach the battlefield is to turn off the A1 and turn north on to the A6094 signposted to Wallyford. About 50 metres down the road there is a monument to the battle at the entrance to a now disused access road on the left, which provides a good parking area. From the monument a good view can be had across Howe Mire towards St. Michael's church at Inveresk. This ground was the scene of the heavy fighting between Angus's division and the English cavalry.

➡ From the monument and How Mire, continue down the A6094 to join the A199 just beyond Wallyford. Follow it into Musselburgh, but do not turn right across the bridge. Instead carry on a short distance to the old bridge and park up. Arran's and Huntly's divisions crossed both this bridge and the immediately adjoining ford before climbing the steep hill towards the church. This area has been extensively built over since the battle, and the area at the top is a curious mixture of municipal cemetery and waste-ground, but nevertheless the extent to which the Scots were in dead ground and quite hidden from Somerset until virtually the last moment is only too apparent. From the church (the present building only dates from 1805) descend the hill again and follow the riverside footpath upstream to find Angus's crossing point - which was probably in the region of Wedderburn House. The river is narrow but has been intensively managed for fishing by building a number of weirs and strengthening the banks. It will have been much shallower and easier to cross in 1547. Once again the degree to which Angus and his men will have been hidden in dead ground until climbing on to Howe Mire is very striking.

**Recmmended Reading:** Oman's account in his magisterial *History of the Art of War in the Sixteenth Century* is perhaps the best known, but is rather unsatisfactory and suffers from having a very poor map and an undue reliance of Ramsay's drawings. Notwithstanding the absence of any maps at all, by far the best modern account is contained in Gervase Phillips' *The Anglo-Scots Wars 1513-1550* (Woodbridge 1999).

# Civil War Battlefields

**Kilsyth** (OS Explorer 349) is easily approached by the A803 from Falkirk, which runs along the southern edge of the battlefield. The *Hollandbush Inn* at Banknock marks Baillie's halting point on the night of 14 August and the bridge at Auchincloch was the scene of his vain attempt to patch a rearguard together afterwards.

At first sight the battlefield appears to lie in an unspoilt rural area, but in fact it is heavily scarred by old mining and quarrying. Many of the small knolls which dot the site are spoil heaps. A significant area – the 'glen' which channelled the initial Royalist advance – has been drowned by a resevoir, and much of the area occupied by Baillie's army is covered by the former mining village of Banton. Nevertheless, even after making due allowance for these deceptive alterations, Baillie's reference to the "impassable ground" describes the field well and it is so broken that visual interpretation is difficult. Much more time than usual needs to be devoted to this battlefield.

➡ The focal point should be the modern village of Banton, which is accessed by turning off the A803 at Kelvinhead. The road between Kelvinhead and the village probably marks the initial position adopted by Baillie's army and it will be immediately apparent that any troops deployed there will have been completely hidden from the Royalists. In addition to the man-made landmarks such as Auchinrivoch Farm, there are a number of significantly named topographical features; Baggage Knowe, Slaughter Howe, and Bullet Knowes which obviously relate in various ways to the battle. The naming of Girnal Hill may also be significant, for girnals were chests used for storing oats and it is just possible that Baillie's pack train may have been left behind here when the army shifted to its right.

The Royalist army was occupying the high meadow immediately below Slaughter Howe, perhaps with their right wing near Colzium Castle, though judging by the state of the ground it is likely they may have been holding a defensive position there rather than lying in ambush.

**Recommended Reading:** There are numerous, largely uncritical biographies of Montrose, but the author's *Campaigns of Montrose* (Edinburgh 1990) and *Auldearn 1645* (Osprey 2003) are still the only military histories of the campaign. Baillie's own account – evidence presented at the subsequent inquiry – has been printed in his kinsman Robert Baillie's *Letters and Journals* (Bannatyne Club 1841-2) and is absolutely essential reading.

**Dunbar** (OS Explorer 351)

➡ Accessed directly from the A1 just to the west of the very prominent cement works. Follow the tourist signs for Doon Hill. The road is narrow and very steep and the surface gradually deteriorates from poor to non-existant. It is quite impassable for coaches. However the road or track eventually leads to a small car park on top of the hill and a quite unparalleled view of the entire battlefield.

Unfortunately some of the more interesting parts of the battlefield have been lost. The roads and the railway, and, with rather less excuse, the cement works have between them effectively destroyed the areas of the initial fighting to secure the Broxburn crossing, and the subsequent cavalry battle. Otherwise however it is unspoiled and of particular interest is the area between Little Pinkerton and the Broxburn which is the likeliest site of the action by Lawers' Brigade. The greater part of the Scots army probably escaped by way of Doon Bridge and just to the west, below Spott Dodd, is the site of the earlier battle of Dunbar in 1296.

**Recommended Reading:** All biographies of Cromwell treat the battle fairly superficially and entirely in accordance with his own self-serving (and totally unreliable) dispatch. The author's *Dunbar 1650* (Osprey 2004) provides a much more detailed narrative, including a full reconstruction of the Scots order of battle.

**Inverkeithing** (OS Explorer 350)
The most spectacularly damaged of all the battlefields discussed in this book, which is a great pity considering how interesting it is. In addition to the inevitable expansion of Inverkeithing itself and the intrusion of Rosyth into the valley between Castland Hill and Pitreavie, the actual battlefield proper has been quite literally cut across by the railway and motorway approaches to the Forth Bridges. Massive rock cuttings have quarried away much of both Holburn's and Lambert's positions, while the narrow neck of land joining them has been filled with equally massive bridges and embankments.

➡ Effectively this is a battlefield which can only be visited by car. Begin by crossing the Forth Road Bridge and as you emerge from the rock cutting on the north side, Castland Hill is on the left, easily identified by two very prominent microwave transmitter masts on top. The road then carries on through Muckle Hill, but a complex of slip roads and roundabouts between the Ferry Hills and Castland Hill overlies the scene of the fighting during the first phase of the battle. Leave the main road (A90) here and take the B980 north along the eastern shoulder of Castland Hill and across the valley now occupied by Rosyth. Join the A823 for a short distance before turning right (east) at the Carnegie Campus and follow the road for approximately one kilometre to Castle Brae on the right. Just beyond the turn-off for Pitreavie Castle is a small memorial cairn to Duart and his men - just north of the crossed swords on the map. Although men eventually stood and died here, this does not of course mark the site of the main engagement. The castle itself is considerably changed, having been substantially reconstructed in 1885 and until recently serving as a NATO headquarters, but some of the original structure remains.

**Recommended Reading:** Unfortunately Inverkeithing remains a forgotten battle and the only real account of it is still to be found in W.S. Douglas's very dated *Cromwell's Scotch Campaign* (London 1898). Firth and Davies' otherwise magisterial *Regimental History of Cromwell's Army* is curiously silent as to most of the regiments which fought there.

# The Jacobite Battlefields

### Sheriffmuir (OS Explorer 366)

➡ Easily accessed from Dunblane and clearly signposted from the Fourways roundabout on the B8033. Proceed up Glen Road as far as 'The Firs', turn left on to the Sheriffmuir Road and carry on as far as the MacRae Monument – a prominent obelisk. There are no formal parking spaces but a convenient niche was been worn in the verge to park a car safely. Alternatively Stirling Council has produced a useful leaflet setting out a walking route, which is estimated as requiring just over an hour from Dunblane Cathedral.

Large areas of the battlefield, particularly on top of the ridge, are now covered in trees and the crossed swords purportedly marking the battlesite on the O.S. map are much too far to the east. However the Sheriffmuir Road, running parallel to and somewhat below the crest of the ridge, almost certainly represents the route taken by Argyle's army on to the battlefield, and by extension may well mark his front line. The slope below it was certainly the scene of a running battle as Argyle's left wing was chased down into the gorge of the Wharry Burn.

In a clearing a short distance from the MacRae Monument is a now recumbent standing stone traditionally known as 'the gathering stone'. While it obviously predates the battle by 1,000 years and more there is no reason why it should not have served as a convenient landmark to attract the Earl Marischal's men on an otherwise featureless ridge, and every reason to suppose therefore that tradition is correct in claiming that it marks the centre of the Jacobite line.

The slope to the north of the gathering stone, by which the Jacobites approached is also heavily wooded, but once over the crest a clear view can be had of both Kinbuck Muir (on the north side of the A9) which is conveniently marked by a rectangular wood, and the adjacent Lower Whitestone farm, which may have been the site of Argyle's final position.

**Recommended Reading:** The most useful military study is John Baynes, *Jacobite Rising of 1715* (London 1970). Despite being readable and well argued it needs to be used with some care since his treatment of the battle of Sheriffmuir is surprisingly superficial and his reconstruction of the Jacobite order of battle contains a number of important errors.

### Prestonpans (OS Explorer 351)

Immediately adjacent to the A1 (which runs along the line of the Tranent meadows) but has been considerably altered by modern developments.

➡ The easiest approach by road is along the A198 which runs parallel to the A1 on the north side of the railway. A stone cairn by the roadside marked only with the legend 1745 is an unusually accurate marker of the approximate position of Cope's right flank. A side-road immediately beside it has a sign pointing to the battlesite - it actually does nothing of the sort, but does lead to a spacious car-park at the Meadowmill sports centre. In laying out the playing fields which lie between the centre and Colonel Gardiner's house the ground level has been lowered considerably and the resulting spoil erected into a high mound which boasts some interpretative boards on top and a good view of the battlefield. Naturally enough the map shows the mound standing well clear of Cope's right flank, although the point is probably immaterial given the presence of the railway line below.

➡ Descending to ground level and moving along the A198 a few metres to the east of the roadside cairn will take the visitor to the still extant track-bed of the Seton Waggonway, along which Cope's army formed in the early hours of 21 September 1745. At the time of writing the fields on either side of the waggonway were still undeveloped and illustrate all too clearly just how flat and open the battlefield really was. The waggonway itself is now a cyclepath and provides a convenient walking route to the church at Tranent, occupied Locheil's men on the day before the battle. On the west side of Tranent is a narrow road variously identified as Birsley Brae and Johnnie Cope's Road which runs down the hill, crosses the A1 by a footbridge and passes by Colonel Gardiner's house to Prestonpans Station. Gardiner's house was called Olive Stob at the time and there is a large obelisk to his memory in the garden on the north side, close by the railway. Sometime afterwards it became Bankton House and after lying in ruins for many years it has been handsomely restored. It is private property.

**Recommended Reading:** The most detailed account available is contained in Professor Christopher Duffy's *The '45* (London 2003), although the present author also unblushingly recommends his own *1745: A Military History* (Staplehurst 1996). Rather dated but still useful is Tomasson and Buist's *Battles of the '45* and the Pan Books paperback edition of 1967 fits very comfortably in the pocket.

### Falkirk (OS Explorer 349)
Relatively unspoilt although the approaches are considerably confused by urban sprawl and by the Forth & Clyde and Union canals on the northern side of the hill.

➡ The best approach is from the A803 which traverses Falkirk. Turn south on to the B816 where it branches off at the point where it crosses the Forth & Clyde Canal near Lock Sixteen. After about a kilometre the B816 turns sharply to the right (west), but you should carry on under a prominent railway bridge and canal viaduct carrying the Union Canal. Ascending a very steep wooded hillside will bring you to the monument just above Greenbank Farm. The road is narrow and surprisingly busy and parking on the verge is not recommended.

The monument is well-sited at the head of the now wooded ravine which protected Hawley's right wing and now provides an excellent reference point for exploring further afield. A long narrow strip of woodland running due south from the area of the monument would appear, inadvertently or otherwise, to mark Hawley's front line at the start of the battle.

**Recommended Reading.** Those books covering Prestonpans also deal with Falkirk, but informed with a wealth of local knowledge Geoff Bailey's *Falkirk or Paradise* (Edinburgh 1996) is superior to all of them put together and will conveniently fit in a jacket pocket.

# Index